Cockatiels

Ellen Fusz

Cockatiels

Project Team
Editor: Mary E. Grangeia
Technical Editor: Tom Mazorlig
Interior Design: Leah Lococo Ltd. and Stephanie Krautheim
Design Layout: Stephanie Krautheim

T.F.H. Publications
President/CEO: Glen S. Axelrod
Executive Vice President: Mark E. Johnson
Publisher: Christopher T. Reggio
Production Manager: Kathy Bontz

T.F.H. Publications, Inc.
One TFH Plaza Third and Union Avenues
Neptune City, NJ 07753

Discovery Communications, Inc. Book Development Team:
Maureen Smith, Executive Vice President & General
   Manager, Animal Planet
Carol LeBlanc, Vice President, Marketing and
   Retail Development
Elizabeth Bakacs, Vice President, Creative Services
Peggy Ang, Director, Animal Planet Marketing
Caitlin Erb, Marketing Associate

Printed and bound in China
07 08 09 10   3 5 7 9 8 6 4 2

Library of Congress Cataloging-in-Publication Data
Fusz, Ellen.
Cockatiels / Ellen Fusz.
p. cm. — (Animal Planet pet care library)
Includes index.
ISBN 0-7938-3766-9 (alk. paper)
1. Cockatiel. I. Fusz, Ellen. II. Title. III. Series. SF473.C6B67 2006
636.6'8656—dc22
2006007720

This book has been published with the intent to provide accurate and authoritative information in regard to the subject matter within. While every precaution has been taken in preparation of this book, the author and publisher expressly disclaim responsibility for any errors, omissions, or adverse effects arising from the use or application of the information contained herein. The techniques and suggestions are used at the reader's discretion and are not to be considered a substitute for veterinary care. If you suspect a medical problem consult your veterinarian.

The Leader In Responsible Animal Care For Over 50 Years!™
www.tfhpublications.com

Table of Contents

Chapter 1

Why I Adore My

Cockatiel

Often whistling, chirping, or singing, cockatiels make wonderful family pets. With their yellow faces and orange cheeks, these friendly and entertaining little mimics look like circus performers. But it's not just their jaunty attitudes that make them a favorite with bird lovers. These beautiful creatures are also highly intelligent. Since they adapt very well to life in captivity, they are often considered almost as domesticated as cats or dogs. Cockatiels are amiable, calm, and good-natured, which makes them ideal for novice or experienced keepers.

The Family Tree

Look to the Australian continent to trace the ancestry of this marvelous avian creature. A member of the parrot group, the cockatiel is part of the same family as the cockatoo. In the animal kingdom, under the classification of Aves, birds are grouped into orders or types. To put it into perspective, the single largest order or type is the passerine, which means perching bird. It is estimated that 50 percent of all birds, over 1,100 species, are passerines. These include canaries, finches, sparrows, robins, buntings, etc.

The cockatiel is a part of another order, the psittacines or hookbilled birds, which contains more than 350 species that includes parrots, parakeets, lories, and cockatoos. Psittacine birds come in all sizes and shapes. Their colors range from a dull brown to the bright, colorful mixtures seen in parrots and macaws. These birds are known for their big heads and their strong beaks. The upper beak, or maxilla, hooks downward, coming to a sharp point. The lower beak, or mandible, curves upward and fits snuggly underneath. This strong bill is an excellent apparatus that they use to climb, dig, and crack open seeds.

The cockatiel, one of over 430 native Australian birds, was discovered when the continent was colonized by Europeans in the late 1700s. Large roosts of wild cockatiels were found in the grassy plains of the interior. Identified as quarrion by the aborigines, flocks were found in the eastern part of the continent, which was then called New Holland. In 1838, English ornithologist and taxidermist John Gould traveled to Australia to catalogue the vast varieties of Australian avian species. During his two year stint, John, along with his wife,

The wild cockatiel originated in Australia. Since his discovery by Europeans in the 1700s, he has gained enormous popularity as a companion bird.

Psittacine or Passerine?

The passerine birds, or perching birds, consist of nearly 300 genera and more than 1,100 species. Some common passerines birds are: canaries, finches, sparrows, robins, grosbeaks, and buntings.

The psittacine birds, or hookbills, are not as diverse, but still contain 80 genera and more than 350 species. The most common psittacines are: parakeets, cockatoos, and cockatiels.

Elizabeth, illustrated and recorded this bird, which he described as the "cockatoo parrot." Later classified as Australian parakeets, these birds were brought back to Europe in the 1840s to be bred as pets. An importer of exotic animals is credited with giving it the name cockatiel, from the Dutch word "kakatielje," which is in turn borrowed from the Portuguese cacatilho meaning "little cockatoo."

As for the bird's eventual scientific classification, this mid-sized psittacine, or hookbilled bird, was given the Latin name, *Nymphicus hollandicus*. Roughly translated, this means, "Dutch nymph," and some claim the designation refers to the painted orange cheeks of a Dutch doll. While this idea is charming, it is more likely that the name refers to the designation of eastern Australia as New Holland.

Physical Characteristics

At maturity, cockatiels weigh in at about 3 to 4 ounces (85 to 113 grams) and average 12 to 13 inches (30.5 to 33 cm) in length from head to tail. The tail makes up half of the body length. This impressive appendage is not simply dragged behind the bird, but it is actively used both during flight and during climbing. When a cockatiel clings to the wire of his cage, you can observe how he spreads his tail and uses it as a prop for balance and support. When the bird walks, the tail is folded tight and held just above the ground.

The cockatiel's crowning glory is his crest, which is made up of many feathers of varying sizes. Breeders often concentrate on this feature to produce varieties with especially prominent and distinguished headgear. The ideal height of the crest is 3 inches (7.6 cm). The longest of these feathers are located at the rear of the crest. It's easy to assess the mood of the cockatiel by the position of the crest. If it is standing upright, the bird is alert and content. But if the feathers are flattened against

An adult cockatiel is about 12 to 13 inches (30.5 to 33 cm) long and has a very attractive, exotic appearance.

cinnamon, pearl, and silver, breeders continue to come up with other mutations for an even wider variety of colors.

When purchasing a cockatiel, perhaps the least expensive and easiest variety to find is the gray. In their native Australian habitat, most cockatiels are this color. These beautiful

the head, it is a sign that the bird is either frightened or angry.

Cockatiels are unusual among psittacines in being dimorphic—the males and females are colored differently. Depending on the color variety, determining the sex of an adult is usually straightforward, but only after the bird is at least six months of age. Medical testing is the only way to be 100 percent positive of the gender of your cockatiel.

Common Varieties

In the wild, most cockatiels are predominantly gray. In captivity, a number of color variations have been derived from the normal gray. While the most well-known are lutino, pied,

Vital Statistics

Size: From head to tail, the wild cockatiel averages 12 inches (30.5 cm) and the domesticated cockatiel averages 13 to 14 inches (33 to 35.6 cm)

Weight: 3 to 4 ounces (75 to 100 grams)

Age at sexual maturity: 6 to 12 months

Average life span: 12 to 15 years

Maximum life span: 20 to 25 years, although there have been reports of some cockatiels living as long as 32 years

little creatures have dark gray feathers covering their bodies. Their wings have prominent white patches, and there is a yellow wash on the face and the crest. Most noticeable are the large dime-sized orange cheek patches, which are stronger in coloration on the male than the female. The bill and the feet are gray, as is the cere—the fleshy patch above the beak where the prominent nostrils are located. The tail is long and tapered, and the underside is barred with yellow and gray. The male and the female look very similar until maturity. At that time, the male feathers become more colorful.

Lutino

A strikingly beautiful bird, the lutino cockatiel is a popular variety. Due to a gene that prevents the formation of melanin, or dark pigment, this cockatiel is white with a yellow wash. The bill and the feet are pink, and the eyes are red. Within this exquisite variety, the male and female look strikingly similar. However, with more careful observation, you can see that the female's tail feathers have a yellow barring, while the males do not.

Pied

Pied cockatiels have large patches of color that can appear anywhere on the body. Some pieds have only an isolated odd white feather, or even just a splotch of pink on the toe. Others are so heavily pied that they appear to be lutinos. It is difficult, if not impossible, to distinguish the male from the female by just looking at the markings.

The normal coloration of wild cockatiels is gray; however, many color mutations abound in captivity. Pictured here are two lutinos and a normal pied.

Dark-Eyed Clear

When a bird looks like a lutino but has the common black eyes, it is usually an extremely heavily pied bird, and it is called a dark-eyed clear. Technically, it is a gray bird covered completely in white patches.

Cinnamon and Fallow

In these birds, two genes have been identified that dilute melanin, or dark pigment, producing brown instead of gray or black. In the cinnamon variety, gray areas are replaced with dark brown. These birds are called cinnamon because their color is sometimes compared to the color of cocoa. The color of the male is somewhat deeper than that of the female. Fallows seem to be a lighter brown than cinnamons, and their eyes are dark red.

Pearl

With a lovely scalloping effect of white edging on each feather of the bird's back and wings, the pearl cockatiel is a festive looking variety. These "pearling spots" are yellow or white and can be found on the back, nape, and wings. On heavily marked pearls, some small yellow or white markings can be found on the breast. Pearling is caused by a gene mutation. It can be combined with other mutations to produce cinnamon pearls, whiteface pearls, etc. Typically, the adult male will lose his pearling after his first molt. An interesting aspect of this mutation is that males have the pearling effect for only about a year, while females retain it for life.

Silver

The silver cockatiel looks like a diluted version of the gray. With red eyes, a pink beak, and pink feet, the male has a deep yellow face and bright orange cheeks. The female tends to be less colorful.

Whiteface

A relatively new variety, the whiteface lacks any yellow or orange coloration. This leaves the face completely white in the male and completely gray in the female. Without the traditional cheek patches, the gray on the body appears to be much stronger, thus causing some to refer to this bird as "charcoal."

Albino

The genetic combination of a whiteface and a lutino may produce an albino, a totally white bird. There is no

Quick Guide to Cockatiel Varieties

Lutino : The lutino is white, with a yellow wash. The bill and the feet are pink, and the eyes are red.

Pied: The pied has white patches that can appear anywhere on the body.

Dark-Eyed Clear: The dark-eyed clear looks like the lutino, but with normal black eyes. It is usually an extremely heavily pied bird.

Cinnamon and Fallow: These cockatiels have brown pigment instead of gray or black. Fallows seem to be lighter than cinnamons, and their eyes are dark red.

Pearl: Pearl cockatiels have a lovely scalloping effect on the back and the wing, with each feather edged in white.

Whiteface: The whiteface lacks any yellow or orange coloration. This leaves the face completely white in the male and completely gray in the female.

Albino: The albino is the genetic combination of a whiteface and a lutino and is a totally white bird.

Rare Varieties: These include the emerald, or olive, which has a decidedly green appearance; the yellowface, which has yellow cheek patches; and the silver, which has a light gray coloration.

Lively and affectionate birds, cockatiels are extremely social, tame easily, and thrive on human companionship.

way to visually discriminate between the male and the female because both sexes are completely white. Once quite rare, these birds are more common now.

Other Varieties

There are other extremely rare varieties, which are bred only by a handful of specialist breeders. These include: the emerald, or olive, which has a decidedly green appearance; the yellow face, or yellow cheek, which has yellow cheek patches; and the silver, which is a silvery-gray with red eyes and a pink beak. The platinum, seen in Australia, has a smoky gray back with an off-white colored chest.

Personality and Temperament

Colorful and appealing, it's hard to resist the playful cockatiel. These little comedians will often do just about anything to get your attention. Cockatiels make wonderful, devoted pets. They have pleasant, sunny dispositions and a lot of personality. Ideal for the first time bird owner, they are usually gentle, loving, and delight in being petted and held. These birds enjoy, and in fact need, time out of their cages to play, exercise, and interact with their owners. Extremely social creatures, cockatiels adore participating in many aspects of your family life.

Life Span

Adolescents: Cockatiels have their first juvenile molt at approximately four months of age. Males begin to acquire more yellow on the face, while females continue to have a less colorful appearance.

Adults: Female cockatiels reach full maturity between eight and ten months of age and can produce eggs at this stage. While a precise age cannot be determined, males begin to show signs of maturity and become interested in breeding after their first full adult molt at one to two years of age. Upon reaching maturity, males have more dominant crests and brighter facial coloration than their female counterparts.

Old Age: In the later stages of your cockatiel's life, he will be less active and perhaps sleep more than he did in the adolescent stage. Make sure your older pet still has time outside the cage to exercise while still getting plenty of rest.

Reaching Old Age: You can help ensure your cockatiel reaches old age and has a long and happy life by providing a clean cage, daily exercise, plenty of companionship and activity, lots of rest, and a healthy diet that includes fresh fruits and vegetables. Your pet should also have a yearly physical examination by your veterinarian to make sure that all is well.

Cockatiels can live as long as 32 years, but their average life span is 12 to 15 years. However, it is not unusual that you may share your home with your feathered pal for 20 years. Here are the physical changes you can expect throughout your bird's lifetime:

Stages of Development

Babies: It is easy to identify a young cockatiel by examining him. The tail feathers are short, and the crest feathers have not fully grown. His body is slimmer, and he has a wide-eyed, innocent look about him. Babies are usually weaned around eight weeks of age.

Battle of the Sexes

In the ongoing battle of the sexes, how do cockatiels fare? Is it a myth that the hens are more affectionate, and only the males will talk? There is certainly a great deal of variation in the nature, behavior, and ability of individual cockatiels. However, gender does play a role in some of these aspects.

Who's the Best?
Vocal ability: males
Whistling: males
Being quiet: females
Hissing and biting: females
Strutting around: males
Best pet: both! (gender is a secondary consideration with these little cuties as you'll more than likely choose the variety of cockatiel before choosing male or female)

These intelligent birds can also be trained to do tricks and to speak. Their vocal abilities are not as great as some parrots, but they excel at whistling. While they can develop a relatively large vocabulary, some cockatiels'

voices aren't the easiest to understand. Males tend to speak and whistle more than their female counterparts. This isn't to say that females can't be taught to speak or won't sing songs; it's just that the males dominate in this arena and are more versatile.

Your Show of Shows

You'll get a kick out of watching your pet cockatiel in action. He'll put on quite a show for you. He is the perfect entertainer. He sings, he dances, and he will make you laugh. You might notice that sometimes your bird will sway from side to side or crouch, flatten his crest, and open his bill menacingly. This is called "dancing." Birds do this for a variety of reasons, including bonding, threatening, dominating, challenging, or simply just for fun. Dancing is often accompanied by shrill, loud calls.

You may sometimes feel as if you are watching an avian Olympics when you observe your cockatiel as he exercises and plays. You'll be amazed by the contortions he performs. Although it may appear that your cockatiel is going to tie himself in a knot, don't worry. It is perfectly normal for him to hang upside down by his feet and pull his head up through his legs. Don't be surprised if he hangs on the underside of the roof of his cage and stretches out his neck as if trying to get down. No need to rush to the rescue, your cockatiel is just playing and having fun.

Not All Fun and Games— But Almost

While cockatiels make almost perfect pets, they do have an annoying behavior that you'll soon learn to take in stride. Cockatiels, like all hookbills, display one practice that can be exasperating. They will often attack their food dishes looking for that "perfect tidbit," flinging seeds and pellets in all directions. Some birds are worse than others, but at times all birds will do this. Aside from the mess, a lot of food can be wasted.

There are several ways of combating this annoying habit to minimize the waste and the mess. One is to offer the various components of the diet in separate bowls—budgie mix in one, pellets in another, etc. Another method worth trying is only partially filling the food dish. This way, the food will fling against the sides of the bowl rather than scatter all over the cage. Some pet stores now carry covered feed dishes that have a hooded top with a front opening.

Another minor drawback to keeping this bird is the housekeeping issue. Cockatiels have a protective coating on their feathers called powder down. But it's not just the feathers that will have the protective coating— everything else in the room can be covered by this fine powder as well. With a little extra dusting during your routine household

Amiable, calm, and playful, cockatiels make ideal pets for novice or experienced keepers.

Before deciding to bring a cockatiel into your home, make sure that you are prepared to offer him the best care possible throughout his lifetime.

Their wide-eyed appearance gives them a look of innocence that is hard to resist. Diminutive fledglings are inquisitive, lively, and eager to explore. They are normally weaned between seven and eight weeks of age. At this point in their development, they are usually friendly and interested in what's going on around them.

Babies can be acquired at pet stores or through breeders. The ideal age for a chick to be purchased is between two and three months of age, as younger birds are easier to train than older ones. When selecting a mature cockatiel, ask about the bird's age and

cleaning, you can easily remove the powdery residue. It is actually a small price to pay for sharing your life with such a loving and responsive pet as the cockatiel.

Selecting Your Cockatiel

When hatched, baby cockatiels are weak and take a long time to develop.

gender. Keep in mind that with some varieties it is difficult to determine sex based upon coloration alone, and that young birds are hard to sex. In some cases, a veterinarian will have to surgically determine if the bird is male or female. Another important question to ask is how he or she was raised.

Cockatiel babies can be raised in

two different ways—nurtured by their parents or handfed by people. This can produce several distinct types of bird. While parent-raised birds are sometimes cautious of humans, they can be tamed to make good pets. But it takes considerable work. Such birds are often considered breeding birds.

When a cockatiel is artificially incubated or taken from the nest and handfed, he will think of the feeder as his parent. He will include all humans in his flock. The baby will be affectionate and cuddly and

The Expert Knows

Attention!

Cockatiels need intellectual stimulation as well as daily companionship. A single bird will do well if you are able to provide the daily attention this pet craves. If, however, you feel that your pet needs more company than you can provide, you might consider getting another cockatiel. With several pet birds, the need for attention is reduced as they have each other for companionship.

Don't think that if you get a pair your job is basically done. Cockatiels still demand attention and need at least several hours each day out of their cages. Since they should never be let out of their enclosures unsupervised, this time can be used to train or to play with your pets. They enjoy riding around on your shoulder, sitting on your finger, or exploring.

will respond to being handled much the same way as a kitten or a puppy. As long as the owner has daily interaction with the bird, he will always remain a trusting and affectionate pet. Because of their social natures, birds accept humans as a part of their flock, and therefore they accept human touch as a part of a bonding or nurturing experience.

Establishing Harmony

Two or more males or females will usually get along well together. It is

FAMILY-FRIENDLY TIP

Cockatiels and Kids

Of course, it depends on the age and temperament of the child, but cockatiels generally make excellent family pets. People of all ages will enjoy watching these playful creatures, especially kids. Since these charming birds love to sing and whistle, they make their presence sweetly known, and they quickly become beloved companions. However, for both the child's and bird's safety, it is recommended that children under the age of eight not handle a cockatiel.

Since the cockatiel's average life span is 12 to 15 years—and many live to 20 years and beyond—having one is a long-term responsibility. Most youngsters will form an attachment to these lively birds, especially if they participate in their daily care. With supervision, youngsters can help their parents with feeding by filling food and water dishes. Older children can take a more active role in overall care and grooming; they can help by preparing the fruit and vegetable part of the diet, and they can assist in maintaining and cleaning the cage.

Having a cockatiel as a family pet is a great way to teach children the correct way to treat a pet, as well as the responsibility of caring for an animal on a daily basis. As the child matures, the level of care and interaction can increase.

The ideal age to purchase a cockatiel is between two and three months, because younger birds are easier to train than older ones.

when you mix the genders that there can be problems. With cockatiels, this is usually not a major dilemma as long as the birds are not breeding. To ensure harmony, there should be an equal number of males and females, and there should be an abundance of nest boxes, as well as careful supervision.

Cockatiels kept together often form a bond or special attachment. You might notice certain behaviors, such as allopreening, which in simple terms means mutual grooming. Birds will typically perch close together and preen each other, especially in the hard to reach areas of the head and neck. This common behavior is a sign of friendship.

Why I Adore My Cockatiel

Chapter 2

The Stuff of

Everyday Life

Now that you have decided on which cockatiel to purchase, you are surely anxious to bring your new pet home. Before doing so, however, it is important that you have everything ready for him when he arrives. This will ensure that his homecoming is as pleasant and stress-free as possible and that your bird will quickly feel comfortable and secure.

The most important piece of equipment you will need for your cockatiel is a proper cage. Since your bird will spend considerable amounts of time in this enclosure, it is important to choose carefully. It isn't enough to select something that shows off the bird to his best advantage. Keep in mind that a cage is a bird's home, and it is essential that it provide the necessary space for him to live a healthy and happy life.

Like most hookbills, the cockatiel uses three forms of locomotion: flying, climbing, and walking. A suitable home should allow your bird to exercise in all three modes. A minimum of 3 feet (0.9 m) in length is needed for a cockatiel to be able to fly from a perch at one end of the enclosure to a post at the other end. If at all possible, it is wise to find a cage that is 4 feet (1.2 cm) in length. The width of the cage should allow the bird to extend his wings and fly. Approximately 18 inches (45.7 cm) is adequate for this activity. Owners might want to check into the availability of flight cages, which are often built to these specifications.

Flight cages are long enough for side-to-side flight and approximately 5 to 8 inches (12.7 to 20.3 cm) wider than your bird's wing span. If you have the space, there are a few good reasons to use such a cage. First, if your bird is going to spend most of his time in an enclosure, you should provide him with as large a cage as possible. Second, a flight cage provides plenty of room for exercise. It is also ideal for breeding birds since flight is a part of the courtship ritual. An alternative to this type of enclosure is a cage designed for small mammals such as ferrets, which often makes a good home for birds as well.

Apart from size, another important consideration is the amount of spacing between the cage bars. Be sure these bars are spaced close enough together

Planning Ahead

Before you bring your cockatiel home, you'll need to have a few supplies on hand to make him feel safe and comfortable when he arrives. The better prepared you are, the smoother the transition will be for your already anxious bird, who will need time to adjust to his new surroundings and family. Having everything in place will make him feel welcome and secure.

The most important piece of equipment you will buy for your cockatiel is a proper cage.

Full-Time Cages

Don't let the term "full-time cage" fool you. It doesn't suggest that your pet won't require out-of-cage activity. It simply means that your pet is going to spend a considerable amount of time in his cage while you are away from home. In order to maintain his physical and mental well-being, a cockatiel needs to be out of his enclosure to exercise and to interact with family members for several hours each day.

If your cockatiel is going to spend the majority of his time in a cage, you will want to make sure that it is spacious and provides the necessary elements every bird needs to function and thrive in a healthy and humane

that your cockatiel can't accidentally get his head or wing stuck.

Types of Cage

There are many types of cage available for your bird. The most important criterion is choosing an enclosure that will provide your cockatiel with a safe and comfortable place to call home.

Responsible Pet Ownership

Pet ownership can be a great way for parents to teach their children responsibility. However, there are a few things to consider when giving over the care of a pet to a child: the age of the child, the child's ability to follow directions and to carry out tasks, and—most important—the overall welfare of the animal. Just because children are of a certain chronological age doesn't mean that they are ready to accept total responsibility for pet care. Parents need to make this determination based on their child's development, but should not give them sole responsibility. Parents must always monitor any tasks to ensure the safety of both the bird and the child.

If caring for the family pet is used to teach responsibility, parents can hang a chart on the refrigerator or family bulletin board. This can help the youngster keep track of necessary daily chores while teaching appropriate care. Each time your child completes the

assigned task properly, you can reward him with a sticker for his efforts; eventually, more responsibility can be granted when enough stickers have been earned. Before handing over full care, the parent should thoroughly explain what is expected. Parents should demonstrate exactly what the job entails. Children often need to be told how to do things more than once. Remember, if a task is well-explained, you stand a better chance of having the child actually do the chore. An example of a good task for a preschooler is filling the water bottle or food dish, but the parent should be the one to place the dish or bottle in the cage. An older child can change the paper on the bottom of the cage, as well as help with feeding.

Above all, parents must supervise until they are sure that the child is able to perform the task correctly. Give encouragement to your child for a job well done.

Cage Safety vs. Design

The best materials for your cockatiel's cage are safe metals and hard plastics. Wooden and antique cages can be dangerous because they are easily destroyed and may harbor bacteria or contain toxins. Buy a cage that will be comfortable for your bird, rather than one that appeals to you because of its design or because it suits your décor. It's important to choose one that is the proper size, shape, and material, so that your feathered companion will have a safe and healthy environment in which to live.

manner. Be cautious of purchasing cylindrical enclosures, which are commonly sold as cockatiel cages. For a full-time cage bird, having such limited space is not only inadequate, but it's cruel. Square or rectangular enclosures are best; they offer much more available space, and birds like to retreat to the cozy corners when they need to feel secure.

Sleeping Cages

If you intend to have your cockatiel spend most of his day out of the cage riding around on your shoulder, or in free flight exploring and looking for mischief around the house, then a small cage may be adequate. His pen would simply be a refuge for eating, sleeping, and quiet time alone. However, do not make the mistake of buying a small enclosure with the intention of keeping your pet free most of the time and later decide to keep him locked up. If your plans should change for any reason, you must purchase a larger cage.

Home-Made Cages

Although most home-made cages are built by breeders or fanciers that keep whole aviaries of birds, there is no reason you cannot make your own cage. If you are looking at this project as a money-saving measure, you will be disappointed. Home-made cages can be quite expensive. The advantage to making a cage is that, as the builder, you have more options and can design an enclosure to your own specifications.

The most serviceable cages are made out of wire mesh, though a combination of wood and wire may also be used. While many other parrots are very adept whittlers, the cockatiel will only nibble on the wood and do some structural damage over time.

There is a great deal of controversy concerning the use of galvanized mesh. Although rare, there have been cases reported of birds allegedly dying from zinc poisoning. Actual laboratory data on appropriate cage materials are hard to come by, and myths and opinions fly freely in the absence of facts.

Aluminum is not suitable for use with cockatiels because it is too soft. There is also always a danger that the birds will chew welded wire, which can cause lead poisoning.

Floor Space

Since cockatiels spend a considerable amount of time on the ground in the wild, the floor area of the cage should be large enough to enable them to walk around in comfortably.

Cockatiels love to walk. A cage roughly 18 inches by 48 inches (45.7 cm by 121.9 cm) would provide ample floor space for a bird to exercise.

Extra Room for Toys

A proper size cage should have plenty of places to attach interesting perches and enough room for objects with which your bird can entertain himself.

You should be able to add a variety of toys to the cage without compromising space for your cockatiel to stretch his wings.

Home Furnishings

Just as your home requires essential items to make it comfortable, so does your bird's cage. Your cockatiel will require a few basic items, such as perches, food dishes, and toys, to make daily life in his cage comfortable and stimulating.

Perches

Once you have purchased the appropriate cage, it's time to furnish it. Hookbills love to climb. They extend their necks, grab hold of perches or bars with their bills, and then pull themselves up. Hanging on with their feet, they repeat the same motions. In

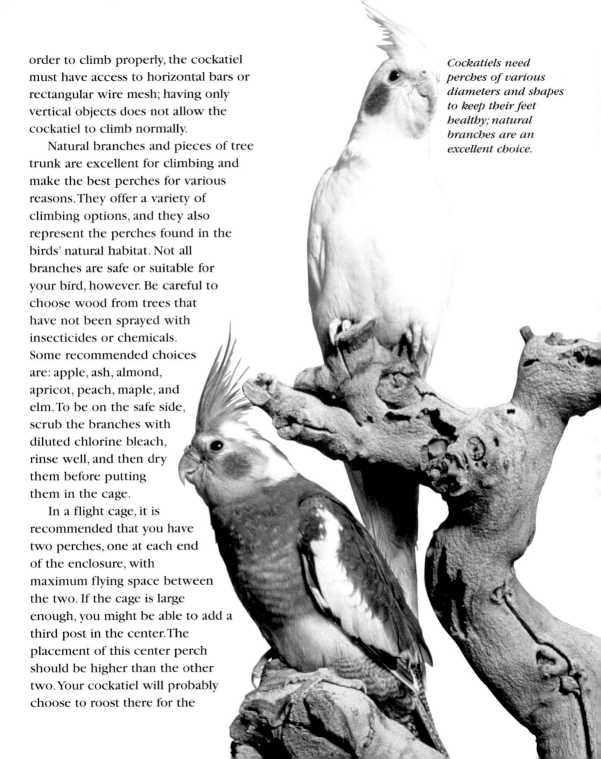

order to climb properly, the cockatiel must have access to horizontal bars or rectangular wire mesh; having only vertical objects does not allow the cockatiel to climb normally.

Natural branches and pieces of tree trunk are excellent for climbing and make the best perches for various reasons. They offer a variety of climbing options, and they also represent the perches found in the birds' natural habitat. Not all branches are safe or suitable for your bird, however. Be careful to choose wood from trees that have not been sprayed with insecticides or chemicals. Some recommended choices are: apple, ash, almond, apricot, peach, maple, and elm. To be on the safe side, scrub the branches with diluted chlorine bleach, rinse well, and then dry them before putting them in the cage.

In a flight cage, it is recommended that you have two perches, one at each end of the enclosure, with maximum flying space between the two. If the cage is large enough, you might be able to add a third post in the center. The placement of this center perch should be higher than the other two. Your cockatiel will probably choose to roost there for the

Cockatiels need perches of various diameters and shapes to keep their feet healthy; natural branches are an excellent choice.

Perfect Perches

Because birds spend so much of their time standing, keeping your cockatiel's feet healthy with varied perch sizes is extremely important. There are many types available: wood, plastic, braided, rope, natural, and even concrete for keeping toenails and beaks trimmed. Wood branches offer a variety of climbing options, and they also represent the perches found in the birds' natural habitat. Not all branches are safe or suitable for your bird, however. Be careful to avoid wood from trees that may have been sprayed with insecticides or chemicals. Apple, ash, almond, apricot, peach, maple, and elm are good choices. To be on the safe side, scrub the branches with diluted chlorine bleach, rinse well, and then dry them before putting them in your cockatiel's cage.

night, as well as use it for a lookout during the day. In a sleeping cage it is common to have a single central perch. The pen is basically a bedroom, so the perch is like the bed.

While there is no defined limit to the number of perches to have in an enclosure, it is important to make sure that flight space is not obstructed. There are perches and ladders of many sizes, shapes, and materials that can give your cockatiel hours of fun. Be careful to avoid the temptation to provide too many roosts, which will crowd the cage thus denying your bird space to excercise and move about.

Wooden dowels of appropriate diameters also make good perches. Because they are made of hardwoods, they withstand the gnawing these birds are known to engage in. Many commercial perches are basically dowels fitted to attach to the cage. Do not use dowels that are covered with sandpaper, however. They are hard on the bird's feet and they harbor bacteria.

Consider providing perches of various sizes and diameters. It is important to give your cockatiel options in the span he must grip with his feet when resting. The various widths will exercise the bird's feet as he perches. Pet birds seem to enjoy standing on a variety of surfaces: some that are very narrow and must be gripped tightly and others that are very broad so that the toes are almost flat against the post. Whichever type of

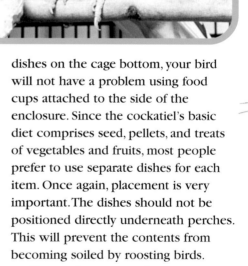

Appropriate cage accessories are essential to your cockatiel's health and well-being.

perch you use, it is vital that they all be securely fastened to the cage. Loose, wobbly, or collapsing posts or branches not only make the bird nervous, but can cause injuries.

Food and Water Dishes

Your cockatiel will need one or more dishes in his cage for food. Most prefer to eat on the floor of the cage, so dishes should ideally be placed there. While it is preferable to have feed

Cage Maintenance Schedule

Daily: Empty and clean food dishes and water bottles.

Every Few Days: Change the paper bedding on the bottom of the cage. You may have to do it daily if you have more than one cockatiel.

Every Week: Clean and disinfect the bottom of the cage.

Every Month: Clean and disinfect the entire cage on a monthly basis. Don't forget that the perches, ladders, and toys must be cleaned and disinfected as well.

dishes on the cage bottom, your bird will not have a problem using food cups attached to the side of the enclosure. Since the cockatiel's basic diet comprises seed, pellets, and treats of vegetables and fruits, most people prefer to use separate dishes for each item. Once again, placement is very important. The dishes should not be positioned directly underneath perches. This will prevent the contents from becoming soiled by roosting birds.

Many avian experts do not recommend using a bowl for water, especially if it is placed on the floor of the cage. Even if you clean it several times a day, it can become extremely dirty. The best device to use is a water bottle. There are several types available at your local pet shop. These glass or plastic bottles are fitted with caps that have metal drinking tubes. The bottle hangs on the outside of the cage, and the metal tube is inserted through the bars into the enclosure. A metal ball at the tip of the drinking tube prevents water from dripping out and causing a mess. The cockatiel drinks by pushing the ball with his tongue, releasing water one drop at a time. Another type of bottle that lacks the metal tube is also available. It hangs on the outside of the cage as well, but the cockatiel has to access the water by sticking his head through a small doorway. The water in these receptacles does get dirty, but not as quickly as in a bowl placed on the floor of the cage.

There is only one disadvantage to using a water bottle. The cockatiel has to learn how to use it! He will naturally dip water out of a dish or bowl, but he won't instinctively know what a water bottle is. The good news is that teaching a bird to use a water bottle is extremely easy. His natural curiosity will work in your favor as you teach him to drink from it. As he discovers how to play with the metal ball in the tube, a drop of water will be released. Even a very slow learner will catch on quickly. If the bird is thirsty, he will react enthusiastically to the sight of the water bottle. In his excitement, he will begin pecking all around to get to the water. When a drop is released, this will positively reinforce the behavior. Often, cockatiel owners report that this is a one-time lesson.

In order to provide fresh food and water in clean receptacles each day, it may be helpful to buy a second set of dishes.

Toy Safety Guide

Aside from being colorful and inviting, toys should be suitable for chewing and pecking. Be sure that all parts, such as beads or bells, are large enough to prevent choking hazards. Scrutinize the links on any item you put in the cage to be certain that your pet cannot become trapped and strangled by them. You should also check to make sure that none of the parts could entrap the bird's feet or toes. With plastic items, look to see that the material isn't brittle and can injure your pet.

Cuttlebones

An important piece of equipment in a cockatiel's cage is the cuttlebone. This accessory not only helps trim the beak, but also provides a source of calcium which your cockatiel needs to maintain good health. Mineral blocks, which are also excellent supplements to your pet's diet, can be placed in the cage as well. Your cockatiel will love to nibble on these vitamin treats.

Creating a Virtual Playground

Just visit your local pet store or go online and you will find that there is a virtual playground available for your pet. One reason there are so many items to choose from is that cockatiels are very playful, and they enjoy having a variety of toys to entertain themselves with in their cages. Before you make a purchase, read the packaging to make sure the item is appropriate for cockatiels. Just as

important as checking information about a child's toy, a conscientious pet owner should read labels thoroughly to ensure that every plaything is safe for his or her pet.

In general, birds love items such as bells, swings, ladders, beads, shiny objects, mirrors, and brass rings. They like colorful things that make noise, and they delight in objects they can chew, hang on to, and swing on. Birds especially need toys that provide them with exercise and fun, while at the same time challenging their minds and bodies. Make sure that all items are made from nontoxic materials and that they are well-constructed and tough enough to endure chewing. Keep in mind that your pet will constantly peck on everything in the cage.

Just as with toys made for kids, the ones made for birds are not meant to last forever either. When cleaning the cage, check to see if any are worn out

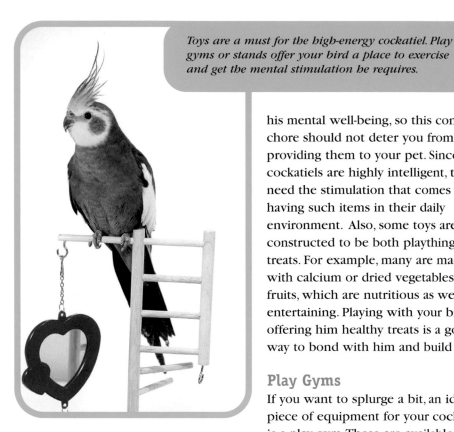

Toys are a must for the high-energy cockatiel. Play gyms or stands offer your bird a place to exercise and get the mental stimulation he requires.

his mental well-being, so this constant chore should not deter you from providing them to your pet. Since cockatiels are highly intelligent, they need the stimulation that comes from having such items in their daily environment. Also, some toys are constructed to be both playthings and treats. For example, many are made with calcium or dried vegetables and fruits, which are nutritious as well as entertaining. Playing with your bird and offering him healthy treats is a good way to bond with him and build trust.

Play Gyms

If you want to splurge a bit, an ideal piece of equipment for your cockatiel is a play gym. These are available free standing or can be attached to the top of most enclosures. Some cages even come with an attached play gym on top. Free-standing gyms allow your bird the opportunity to climb and play on structures that are too large to fit inside his cage.

They can be as simple as a T-perch with a couple of toys attached, or as complex as a wood and plastic multi-level playground, complete with ladders, ropes, toys, food dishes, swings, and any other apparatus used for exercise and fun. They need not bc

and need to be replaced. Most pet toys are inexpensive and should be thrown away when they begin to show obvious signs of wear. Your cockatiel will enjoy the stimulation that comes from having new playthings in his enclosure.

Another thing to remember is that it's important to keep all toys extremely clean. These items can become soiled with feces and should be attended to on a regular basis to maintain your bird's good health. As mentioned earlier, toys are essential for

Homemade Toy Alternatives

If you enjoy craft projects, you can have a lot of fun inventing playthings for your pet. Not only are homemade toys inexpensive to make, but they also offer you a special way to bond with your precious bird.

Most pet stores have an abundance of affordable supplies that you can use to create your own toys. You can find ropes of twisted cotton and leather or chains made of plastic or metal. With hook links made of plastic or stainless steel, you can string a variety of wooden beads, metal bells, plastic jingle balls, or rings together to make colorful baubles for your cockatiel to enjoy. You can also purchase kits that contain many of these items.

The most important thing to remember is that all of the parts you use are safe for cockatiels. They should be the right size to prevent choking or injury. If children participate, be sure to check that the toys they made have been well-constructed for your bird's safety. Creating toys can be a fun family activity that can also be used to teach kids about cockatiels and their care.

expensive or elaborate. A branch pruned from an apple tree that is firmly attached to the top of the cage can provide a multitude of climbing, hanging, perching, and chewing options for your cockatiel. If you have several cockatiels, you might investigate the possibility of purchasing one of the more elaborate play gyms. These often have wheels on the base making them easy to move around your house. Another important feature of this type of setup is the droppings tray, which makes cleanup easier.

The play gym is a great piece of equipment, and it can easily provide your cockatiel with much needed physical and mental stimulation. It is also a handy contraption because it can distract your bird while you are cleaning his cage or taking care of other chores. A full-flighted bird will often spend a good deal of time on the gym, while a clipped bird may stay on one for several hours. But remember, any bird can climb off and start wandering. Always monitor your cockatiel when he is out of the cage. For safety, you should never leave your bird unsupervised under any circumstances.

Bedding/Substrate

The type of bedding you use on the bottom of your cockatiel's cage is important—not just for cleanliness, but for your pet's overall health as well. The most practical bedding material is newspaper. It is inexpensive, readily accessible, and therefore the substrate of choice. Because paper is less likely to support bacterial growth, your bird is less prone to get sick from bacterial infections. It is also easier to check for changes in your cockatiel's stools, which can sometimes be an indication of a health problem.

The disadvantage of newspaper is that you often have to fit it to the size of the cage bottom. It is also important to use just black and white print. Color print contains chemicals that can be harmful to your bird. Other choices to line the cage with are paper towels, wax paper, or paper grocery bags.

Some people mistakenly think that corn cob, sand, pine shavings, or kitty litter can be used to cover the bottom of the enclosure, but these are potentially hazardous to your bird. They can cause impactions should the bird

eat these materials. Also, because they are often breeding grounds for bacteria, they need to be changed daily for optimum health.

Cage Covers

Some cockatiel owners place a cover over the cage at night, while others feel that this is unnecessary. In the wild, the protective cover of trees and branches forms a natural canopy over the bird,

Covered and Cozy

Although some birds become frightened in the dark, others like to be covered at night. An appropriate cover can help eliminate nighttime drafts and will allow your cockatiel to sleep longer in the morning. In the wild, birds need 10 to 12 hours of shuteye a day and should get about the same amount in the home. Try experimenting by covering the cage, and see how it goes. The most important determining factor will be how your bird reacts to it.

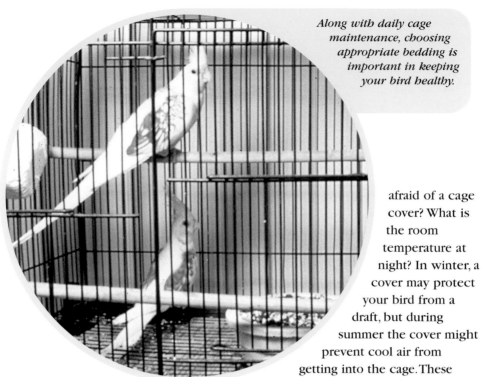

Along with daily cage maintenance, choosing appropriate bedding is important in keeping your bird healthy.

thus providing him with a cozy, secure place to sleep. Since some birds need as much as twelve hours of slumber, an owner may cover his bird's cage to imitate the warm and comforting covering a bird would seek in his natural habitat. What should a cockatiel owner do? There is no single correct answer to this question.

There are a number of factors that a bird owner should consider. Does the room get dark enough at night? Is there an outdoor light source streaming through the window that would cause the room to have more brightness than normal for nighttime? Is your bird afraid of a cage cover? What is the room temperature at night? In winter, a cover may protect your bird from a draft, but during summer the cover might prevent cool air from getting into the cage. These questions should be examined to determine whether a cover is beneficial or not.

Try experimenting by covering the cage, and see how it goes. The most important determining factor will be how your bird reacts to it. Remember that birds nap during the day when the cage is uncovered, so it is not impossible for them to get a good night's rest without being covered. If you need to cover the cage at night for any reason, and your cockatiel seems frightened by it, try starting out by covering just half of it and gradually work your way up to covering the entire enclosure.

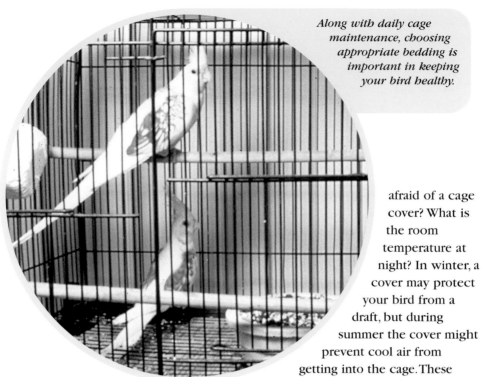

Along with daily cage maintenance, choosing appropriate bedding is important in keeping your bird healthy.

Seed Catchers

Many cages come with a built-in seed catcher. If not, you can purchase one that clips to the side supports of the cage or the front or back handle of the pullout tray. If your bird drops seeds outside the cage, they will be redirected back into the pullout tray thus eliminating a mess on the floor.

Grooming Supplies

Most cockatiels love to bathe, and this is an important part of their care. If you go to your local pet store, you can purchase a relatively inexpensive birdie bathtub. There are many varieties available. Some of the little tubs have mirrors on the bottom. This is to encourage your bird to play in the water longer and get really wet. You can also use a dish you already have. A large, open container or pie pan (glass, not aluminum) set on the floor of the cage makes a good birdbath. It should be shallow enough that your cockatiel can stand in it without the water rising above his belly.

Many pet stores carry perches that you can attach to the shower in your home. While this might be appropriate for some parrots, it is not always recommended for

cockatiels. Before you buy such a perch, talk to your vet.

Cockatiels should be misted daily, or at least several times a week. In the wild, cockatiels enjoy the mist from rain, which not only cleanses them but is a refreshing treat as well. Your local pet store carries mist bottles. You can also purchase them at any department or hardware store.

Beak and Nail Trimmers

There are a number of pet supplies you can purchase to help keep your bird's nails and beak trimmed. You can place pumice perches and lava stones in the cage. These both provide opportunities for natural beak and nail trimming, which is preferred.

Nail clippers and scissors are also available at most pet stores. Before purchasing these supplies, make sure

Bathing is a natural behavior for birds and should be encouraged by providing your cockatiel with a birdbath.

Bird Spa

Putting a special suction-cupped perch on your shower wall is a great way to spend more time with your cockatiel and gives him a steamy spa treatment that's great for his feathers and skin. Be careful, however, to prevent him from getting burned by keeping the water temperature on the cooler side in case he inadvertently flies into the stream. Close the toilet lid, closet doors and windows, and never leave him unattended. Put him back into his cage if you're going to use a blow dryer or flat iron, as both may contain nonstick elements that can cause noxious fumes. Also, it's always a good idea to check with your vet before trying this or anything new to be sure it is suitable for your cockatiel.

that they are the right size for a cockatiel. It's also a good idea to have your vet or breeder show you how to use them appropriately before attempting to groom your bird for the first time. Styptic powder or pencils are important to have on hand to stem any bleeding should you clip a nail too short.

Housekeeping Supplies

While there are no hard and fast rules regarding how often a cage should be cleaned, it is important to establish a routine for such housekeeping matters. There are a number of factors that may determine the frequency of cage cleaning. Obviously, if you have more than one bird, you will need to clean the cage more often. If your bird spends most of his time in the cage, you will need to clean it more frequently as well. Your pet's health is directly related to keeping his environment sanitary. It's not enough just to change the bedding on the bottom of the cage. The floor should be washed at least once a week. The entire enclosure should be cleaned with disinfectant on a regular basis. It is recommended that this be done at least once a month.

Most household cleaners and disinfectants can be harmful or toxic to your bird, and therefore are not suitable for use in a bird cage. There is one exception — good old-fashioned chlorine bleach. Mixed according to label instructions and properly rinsed from the enclosure and furnishings, bleach is fairly safe. It is, after all, basically the same as the chlorine added to municipal drinking water and swimming pools. Again, it's important to note: Bleach is safe when mixed according to label instructions and properly rinsed off surfaces. Bleach is not safe (for you or your bird) when used on aluminum surfaces, as this could produce harmful gases. Due to its soft nature, aluminum is also unsafe for birds because it can be toxic if it is chewed and ingested.

Your pet store may carry a disinfectant formulated especially for birds. Do not use any product that is intended for animals other than birds, as they can be poisonous. For example, a cleaner used in a kennel would be toxic to birds.

When cleaning your cockatiel's cage, remember it's not just the cage that needs cleansing. Toys, ladders, swings, and perches should be scrubbed as well. If you feed your bird soft moist foods, the bowls need to be cleaned each time they are used. It is an opportune moment when cleaning these items to examine them for chips, broken parts, etc.

Location, Location, Location

Just as in real estate, location is a major factor in determining the desirability of any home. The placement of your bird's cage, too, is extremely important in keeping him healthy and content. There are some specific guidelines to follow when deciding where to put your cockatiel's home.

First and foremost, find an active area in your house where your pet will be part of daily family life. Cockatiels thrive on attention, and it is important to have them housed where they can receive the tender, loving care that they crave. Look for a spot away from windows or doors. Drafty areas can cause the bird to become sick. Don't forget that ceiling fans can be drafty as well. It's also best to avoid placing the cage directly in front of a heating or air-conditioning vent. It's vital to keep the cage away from areas where

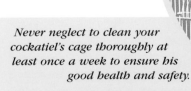

Never neglect to clean your cockatiel's cage thoroughly at least once a week to ensure his good health and safety.

perfumes, hairsprays, or air fresheners are plugged in or sprayed. Some of these products contain chemicals that can be toxic to your bird. It is also important to note that the heating elements in some appliances and certain types of cookware give off toxic fumes that can be fatal to birds without warning.

Safety Concerns

If you choose to let your cockatiel have free reign of the house during the day, it is vital that you take certain precautions. Just as families child-proof rooms from wandering toddlers, a bird owner must do the same. Perform a visual inspection of your house keeping a bird in mind. Try to examine each room from your cockatiel's point of view. Remember, these are curious creatures that love to investigate and play.

Start at the top of a room and work your way down to the floor. For example, if you have a ceiling fan, this

Birdie Daycare

Cockatiels thrive on attention, and it is important that they receive the tender, loving care that they crave. So, like most owners, you have to come up with various ways to keep your bird content and entertained while you're away from home. You can leave the television or radio on to keep him company as silent environments tend to make birds nervous. You can also keep your cockatiel entertained by providing him with a variety of toys in his cage. Change the toys frequently so that your bird will have constant mental stimulation.

Also, remember that the placement of your bird's cage is extremely important in keeping him healthy and happy. There are some specific guidelines to follow when deciding where to put your cockatiel's home. Your bird will do best being in an active area in your house where he will be part of daily family life.

could present a potentially lethal hazard. Check to see that any window coverings or curtains do not have sharp, exposed hooks or pins. Make sure that windows are adequately locked or have screens on them to prevent the bird from getting out of the house. Be sure that there are no poisonous house plants in the area he'll be exploring out of his cage. The following is a partial list of plants that are poisonous to birds: dieffenbachia, elephant ear, lily of the valley, Jerusalem cherry, philodendron, poinsettia, and rhododendron. Cut flowers such as irises, daffodils, and peonies are also toxic.

The kitchen is an area that needs special consideration. Make sure that the stove is turned off when your bird is free. When cooking meals, be careful that your pet is safe and out of the area. Leaving the sink full of water can spell disaster for any bird left unattended. Even a pan filled with dishwater can be harmful to your cockatiel because these birds love the water. If they plunge into these places, their feathers can become saturated, causing them to drown. Pans of hot water or hot cooking oil left on the stove can be lethal. Nonstick cookware, especially if it is overheated, can emit fumes that are deadly to birds. Naturally, you wouldn't overheat a pan on purpose, but accidents do happen. In addition, many authorities now feel that any use of nonstick cookware should be avoided. Err on the side of caution: don't use nonstick cookware if you keep birds.

Certain foods are harmful or toxic to your bird, so be wary of anything that may be left out. Chocolate, avocados, coffee beans, potatoes, tea, salt, and alcohol are just some of these. To be on the safe side, keep all foods covered. Cockatiels tend to peck at unfamiliar substances they encounter during their explorations. In a moment's notice, they can get into trouble.

Your cockatiel needs to feel like part of the flock, so his cage should be placed in an active area where he can participate in daily family life.

Bird-Proofing Tips

Before letting your cockatiel out of his cage, it's important to bird-proof your home. First and foremost, make sure that he will be unable to fly out of the house by keeping all windows and doors closed while he is roaming about. The curious cockatiel loves to explore, so be sure to take a look at every room he'll have access to keeping this in mind. Take care that your pet is safe from things like poisonous plants, ceiling fans, plug-in air fresheners, uncovered toxic foods, pots cooking on the stove, cleaning supplies, and sharp objects.

Another thing to consider is any possible drowning hazard. A sink, bathtub, or an open toilet full of water can pose a lethal threat. Birds fly in for a look, or for a bath, and may not be able to get out because of steep, slippery surfaces. The unexpectedly deep water can also saturate their feathers, making it impossible for them to fly. In a panic, they can quickly succumb.

The curious cockatiel will nibble on just about anything he encounters. When he chooses to chew on something like an electrical cord, the outcome can easily lead to death. Be sure all electrical wires and appliances are placed out of reach.

Don't assume your other family pets have accepted your cockatiel and not harm him. It is easy to be lulled into a false sense of security if the family pets have co-existed together in harmony for some time. Sometimes, for some inexplicable reason, the other family pet can attack your bird. Cockatiels don't stand a chance against most housepets.

To prevent harm from coming to your bird, always supervise him when he is out of the cage. Never leave him unattended under any circumstances.

Although this is overstating the obvious, cockatiels should be in a smoke-free environment. Tobacco and cigarette smoke is a serious assault on the delicate respiratory system of your bird. When you are working on home projects, such as painting, make sure that your bird is well away from the fumes. As mentioned earlier, but worth repeating, plug-in air fresheners and scented candles should be avoided.

In general, it is important to always supervise your cockatiel whenever he has free roam of the house. Just as you would watch a young child, cockatiels should never be left unattended.

Chapter 3

Good Eating

When the question "What's for dinner?" pops into your mind, you might not be thinking about what you'll feed your pet cockatiel. You're probably just contemplating your family's evening meal. You may be familiar with the food pyramid or other nutritional guidelines to keep your loved ones healthy. When planning the family menus, you want to provide a variety of foods high in nutrition that are also appetizing and delicious. The same thought that goes into preparing meals for your family should be given to feeding the family pets.

P lanning meals for your pet takes more thought than just scooping out some bird seed and filling a dish. It doesn't have to be time-consuming or expensive, but when feeding your bird, nutrition should be a top priority.

Determining what to feed your cockatiel can be challenging. Since a well-balanced diet is the foundation of good health for humans and animals alike, it is of the utmost importance that what you feed your bird will contribute to his good health. As can be expected in the area of nutrition, there are several points of view as to the best way of providing your bird with these needed elements.

In the wild, the natural diet of cockatiels is largely made up of seeds, which provide some protein, vitamins, and a lot of carbohydrates. They eat fruits and vegetables, including leaves, stems, flowers, roots, and bark, as well as some insects in small quantities. With an abundance of foods available to these birds, a wild cockatiel's diet is properly balanced.

In captivity, however, it is up to the bird owner to provide a nutritious diet for optimum health. Just as with humans, the basis for good health starts at the table; and in the animal world, the same principle holds true. The soundness and longevity of your bird can in part be attributed to what he is fed. It isn't always immediately apparent that a bird is suffering from a poor diet. Usually, by the time you notice that there is something wrong, the bird is already seriously ill. Poor nutrition can cause susceptibility to disease, as well as lack of energy and vitality.

A nutritious and well-balanced diet is crucial to maintaining your bird's health.

Seeds can make up a large portion of your cockatiel's diet as long as they are supplemented with other healthy foods.

A common sense approach to feeding your cockatiel is important. While there isn't a food pyramid for birds as such, you can get an idea of what you should serve your pet by examining the nutrients a cockatiel would have in his natural environment.

In the wild, a natural, well-balanced diet will contain the following food groups: grains, fruits and vegetables, and animal protein. Another vital part of your bird's sustenance comes from water. It is imperative that a bird have fresh water on a daily basis.

There are several ways of providing a good substitute for the cockatiel's natural diet. These options fall into two groups: seed-based diets or a pellet-based regimen.

Variety

Birds are like humans in their dietary needs and require the same nutrients to be healthy. You can get an idea of what you should serve your cockatiel by examining what he eats in his natural environment. In the wild, his diet is largely made up of seeds, fruits, and vegetables. The key to his optimum health is variety. A balanced diet can make the difference between poor health and good health.

Seed-Based Diets

A good budgie seed mix (white millet and canary seed) can make a healthful foundation for a cockatiel's diet, but seeds alone will not sustain your pet. Cockatiels kept on a diet of only seeds are prone to disease and are destined

Feeding Schedule

Twice Daily: Change water, and clean the water bowl or bottle twice daily for optimum good health.

Daily: Cockatiels need a staple diet of fresh seeds or pellets daily. In addition, they should be offered fresh fruits and vegetables every day.

Once a Week: Feed your cockatiel a hard-boiled egg once a week.

to die prematurely. Seeds do not have all of the nutrients that your cockatiel needs. They are lacking in certain vitamins and minerals, and even high-protein seeds and grains do not offer sufficient amino acids. In the wild, these sources of protein are provided by the ingestion of insects that birds consume during their daily foraging. In captivity, you can provide the additional source of protein by feeding your cockatiel cooked poultry and eggs. The entire egg is good for your pet. You should serve small pieces, shell and all. Cockatiels enjoy

scrambled eggs as well. Since eggs are high in fat, they should be served sparingly, perhaps once a week.

A bird's intestinal tract is not adapted to digest dairy products. Cockatiels should not have milk, but an occasional bit of cheese is not a problem. However, it should never become a staple in your pet's diet. Since many cockatiels love to nibble on pizza, they may get a bit of cheese. Just make sure that a cockatiel's pizza party is a rare occasion.

Although commercial budgie, lovebird, and cockatiel seed mixes are quite good, many are a bit monotonous. Cockatiels enjoy other seeds and grains, such as oats, sunflower seeds, safflower seeds, rye, wheat, and wild seedling grasses. A favorite among many cockatiels is a raw ear of corn. Sunflower seeds are like candy to a cockatiel. The birds love them, but they can only handle a few of them at a time due to their high fat content. It is best to reserve sunflower seeds for treats and rewards.

Pellet-Based Diets

Today, there are pellet diets available formulated specifically for cockatiels and other parrots. A great deal of research has gone into these products, and they provide an excellent nutritional base. Many bird owners use pellets as the basis for their pets' diets and feed no seed at all, or give seeds only as a treat.

Some owners think that a pellet-based diet is more expensive than a seed-based regimen. Pellets do cost more per pound, but they cut way down on waste. Because there are no hulls, the entire pellet is edible. Of course, since cockatiels, like parrots, are messy eaters, there is some waste even with pellets. As the bird chews them they crumble, and the bird will ignore the smaller pieces.

Pellets are usually labeled "nutritionally complete," but many bird breeders disagree. They say that cockatiels need supplementary feeding to thrive. Most experts agree that pellets provide more of the nutritional needs for these birds than seeds. The only drawback is that many cockatiels refuse to eat pellets at first.

Switching From Seeds to Pellets

When a cockatiel is handfed and weaned to an extensive variety of foods, including pellets, he is well on his way to

a long, healthy life. If he started out on a seed diet or has been on seeds for a long time, he may refuse to eat pellets. It is not that the cockatiel dislikes pellets; the bird simply doesn't recognize them as food.

Some owners have success mixing the pellets with the seeds and gradually changing the proportions until the seeds are eliminated completely. Unfortunately, what usually happens is that the bird picks out the seeds and gets hungrier by the day. Having your bird observe another bird eating the pellets is the fastest way to train him. But if you don't have another bird, you can pretend to be the other bird. No,

Pellets, seed mixes, and nuts are nourishing and beneficial, but no one food source can provide for all of your bird's nutritional needs.

Diet Change Caution

If you decide to convert your cockatiel from one type of diet to another—for example, from a seed-based diet to a pellet-based diet—consult with your avian veterinarian first. Conversion can be stressful, and your bird should be in prime condition before you make the switch. Although cockatiels are not known to be picky eaters, they get used to a steady diet quite readily. As a result, it may be difficult to get them to eat properly if their food regimen is suddenly changed.

you don't have to actually eat the pellets. Just make believe that you are enjoying them, and offer to share the pellets with your bird. Another technique that might work is adding your bird's favorite treat to the pellets. In any case, do not give up. With persistence you can eventually get your cockatiel to accept the pellets.

Supplementing Seed or Pellet Diets

Whether you choose a seed- or pellet-based plan, you will need to supplement this diet with fruits and vegetables. Keep in mind that seeds and pellets are just one part, although a significant part, of your cockatiel's nourishment. Think of this staple as the main course of the meal. However, it is often the side dishes on the menu that are the tastiest.

Variety—The Spice of Life

Just as we enjoy variety in our diets, birds are no exception. A varied menu

is stimulating as well as pleasurable for your pet. Cockatiels eat better when they don't get the same thing for every meal. Many bird owners find that their cockatiels have more robust appetites when they have changing menus at mealtime.

Pet food manufacturers realize this fact and try to provide an assortment of foods rather than just one type. Companies that manufacture pellets try to provide the variety a cockatiel needs by making the pellets different colors, shapes, and flavors. You can also purchase a blend of seeds to offer your bird at mealtime. Whether it is pellet or seed, the diversification comes from the supplementary foods you add to his diet. It's not hard to find daily variety with all of the foods that are good for your cockatiel to eat.

Fruits and Vegetables

Cockatiels need a daily intake of fresh fruits and vegetables. Seeds don't provide the vitamins contained in fruits

Picky Eater Problem Solver

Sometimes, getting your bird interested in eating certain foods, like veggies and fruits, can be tricky. Try chopping, grating, slicing, or offering the food whole. Clipping greens to the side of the cage is a great way to get your bird interested in them. A "birdy kabob" is a great way to get your little feathered friend to eat. Simply thread small bits of vegetable and fruit onto the kabob and hang it in the cage. This gives your cockatiel the feeling of having to "work" for his food, which is a natural behavior in the wild.

Be patient. Offer new things week after week. Cockatiels are curious by nature and will eventually try the new food. If your bird is still fussy after a few weeks, perhaps it's because he's afraid of the dish you're using, or he's not happy with the way you're offering the food. Perhaps the food is too big or too small. Change the dishes. Cook the vegetables. You can even bake or cook fresh veggies and fruit into breads, casseroles, and other meals. If you're pressed for time, you can use frozen vegetables and fruits — they aren't as good as using fresh produce, but if that's all you have time for on a particular day, they are better than nothing.

Fresh fruits and vegetables should be a daily staple in your bird's diet.

and vegetables, so it is up to you to make sure your bird has them on a daily basis. They enjoy vegetables high in carotene such as sweet potatoes, carrots, yams, corn, spinach, and red peppers. They also enjoy turnips, green beans, peas, corn, tomatoes, and beans. Fruits such as strawberries, melon (fruit and seeds), apples, oranges, peaches, bananas, watermelon, etc. also are important elements in the cockatiel's diet. Dark green leafy vegetables such as broccoli, spinach, kale, and collard greens have excellent nutritional value. The more color the better. For example, romaine lettuce provides more vitamins than iceberg lettuce, which offers little in terms of nutrition. Remember, variety is the key.

Eggs

If you've heard the expression "eggs are nature's perfect food," it doesn't just apply when referring to a human diet. Eggs are also a perfect food for your cockatiel. While they shouldn't be used on a daily basis because they contain too much fat for your pet's sustenance, as a regular treat they can't be beat. They are easy to feed, either scrambled or hard-boiled. Don't forget that the shell contains nutrients that should be included in the snack.

Table Foods

Within reason, what's good for you is good for your bird. There are a couple of exceptions — dairy products, fatty foods, sugary foods, chocolate, and avocados. The major problem with table foods comes from the fact that many people eat foods that are not good for them.

Another factor to keep in mind is a human's size versus the size of a cockatiel. Your body can tolerate small amounts of caffeine, sugar, salt, grease, and alcohol. A limited amount will have a negligible affect on you. But you easily outweigh your bird by a couple hundred times or more. That means that the negligible effect of caffeine in a piece of chocolate on your body could very easily translate into an overdose for your cockatiel. For your cockatiel to eat one

The Expert Knows

Dietary Supplements

Vitamins can be added to your bird's diet. They come in two forms: liquid and powder. The powdered form can be sprinkled on fruits and vegetables or in the seed mix. The liquid is added to the drinking water. While the liquid is a good source for vitamins, it forms a scum in the water bottle. It is essential to keep the water container clean and filled with fresh water. Always follow the directions on the package because too many vitamins can cause serious health problems. While some birds need grit or gravel to aid digestion, cockatiels do not need grit since their gizzards are able to grind their food. It was once thought that grit could be given in small doses a couple of times a year. However, it is now known that giving even a pinch on a rare occasion can be hazardous to a cockatiel's health.

Foods to Avoid

While there are many human foods that your cockatiel can enjoy, there are some that are potentially hazardous or even fatal. The following foods should be avoided: avocados, chocolate, salt, alcohol, caffeine, and milk.

salty, greasy potato chip could be the equivalent to you eating several bags of them. Play it safe — don't give your bird coffee, tea, chocolate, colas, alcoholic beverages, or extremely greasy or salty foods.

If your pet has free flight or you let him out of the cage during mealtime, he will more than likely join you at the table. This is an excellent way of getting your bird to try new foods.

When feeding "human foods," make sure to serve only bird-sized portions and serve only foods that are safe for cockatiels.

baked potato or that serving of broccoli can be put to good use, too. Your cockatiel will love these special tidbits and love you for giving them to him! However, never serve food that is moldy or spoiled.

Besides fruits and vegetables, your cockatiel will enjoy various grain products, which are perfect for your pet. Whole-grain breads and pasta, brown rice, oatmeal, cornmeal porridge, wheat bulgur, and couscous are just the beginning of the tempting morsels to which he could be introduced. There is nothing wrong with refined foods like regular pasta or rice, but just as for humans, the whole grain varieties are far more nutritious.

Many food scraps are good for your bird as well. Vegetable parings, over-ripe fruit, or stale whole-grain bread are all potential bird food. That leftover

Water—The Most Important Element of All

All living things depend on water. It provides essential nutrients, aids digestion, helps the body absorb vitamins and minerals from food, and aids in waste elimination.

For optimum health, birds require fresh water several times a day. Ideally, the water bottle or dish should be changed twice daily. If you neglect this important task, your bird could be at risk for some health problems. Bacteria can grow at an alarming rate and this, of course, can cause illness in your pet. Many people get into the habit of changing the water first thing in the morning and then once again in the evening.

Proper Food Preparation

We all know that before we prepare food we should start by washing our hands. It's an easy thing to forget when we get busy and have a lot to do. We might even rationalize that we're just preparing food for our pet, and it isn't as necessary. Animal or human, it is extremely important to wash before and after handling food and handling animals. It is easy to spread disease unintentionally by neglecting this very important first step.

Home Cooking

You don't have to be a culinary genius to provide some delicious home-cooked foods for your cockatiel. Some simple bread or soup mixes can be the basis for luscious treats for your pet. It's a good way to ensure that your cockatiel is getting the sustenance he needs for good health.

Rice, Beans, and Pasta

Perhaps you have seen those 15-bean mixes sold for soup in the grocery store. They are perfect for your cockatiel. Add brown rice, wheat, and pasta to get an even more varied food. Since there is no correct mixture, and most bird owners make it a little different each time, it's a great way to be creative in the kitchen. Any

Food Safety

Wash all fruits and vegetables thoroughly before serving them to your cockatiel. His body is small and can be affected by even the tiniest traces of pesticides. Offer organic produce if you can, so that you have one less thing to worry about. Fruits and vegetables sour quickly in warm weather, so remove them a few hours after you offer them and replace them with a new batch at this time if that's convenient. You can leave these foods with the bird longer in cooler weather, but make sure to remove them in the evening. Also, many experts believe that bacteria can contaminate seeds. For absolute safety, owners can microwave seed mixtures before feeding them. Microwave them on high for 5 minutes, stirring once.

legumes and grains can be combined. Cover the mix with a couple of inches of water, bring to a boil for several minutes, and then let it cool. Refrigerate it overnight before draining, and the seeds will be plump and juicy. A batch of bean mixture can be frozen in single serving portions and thawed out when needed.

Cooked bean and rice mixtures can be the staple food in a healthy diet for your cockatiel instead of pellets or seed mixtures. Fed daily, they provide a great deal of nutrients your bird needs and in a very palatable form. Generally, these mixes are cooked until barely tender, both to conserve the nutrients and to give the bird more of a crunch rather than a soft mush when he bites into it.

Bird Bread

If you enjoy the smell of fresh bread baking, think of making some bird bread for your pet. Like bean mixtures, there are many bird bread recipes available. Many of these breads are made of basic cornmeal with the addition of other foods. Not only are they delicious, but they are also a great way to use leftovers. You can use whole wheat flour, rolled oats, or some of the exotic flours such as ground rye, spelt, amaranth, millet, soybean, etc. Mix several cups of the flour or meal with a tablespoon of baking powder. Add two or three eggs (shells and all). Blend these ingredients with some honey or sugar and enough water to make a batter. Add leftover vegetables, grate in a few carrots, or add a can of corn. Bake the mixture until golden brown. Cool and then serve.

Clean, fresh water should be available to your cockatiel at all times.

The Ideal Spot for Food Dishes

The most important thing to remember when placing food dishes in the cage is to make sure that your cockatiel has easy access to these containers. While some people hang dishes from the side of the cage, others place the dishes on the floor. In either case, ask yourself the following two questions:

Can my bird access his food easily?

Is there any danger of bird droppings falling into the food dishes? These factors will determine proper placement. Avoid putting perches in a position where droppings may fall into food. It is also important to remove food that has been contaminated by droppings immediately. Bacteria can grow at a rapid rate, and spoiled food can make your pet ill.

Birds love to eat this bread. They enjoy poking around to find the hidden "goodies" (vegetables) in it.

You can buy processed cornmeal at the store, or you can use fresh-ground cornmeal. The commercial variety has the germ removed and will therefore not become rancid very quickly. If you use fresh-ground, keep it refrigerated and use it within a few days.

Sprouts

Cockatiels enjoy any sprouted seed or grain. Sprouted wheat is an excellent choice, and even a wildbird seed mix will make a tasty sprout. Most cockatiels go for sprouted sunflower seeds even more aggressively than they go for the dry seeds.

The only concern when feeding your bird sprouts is mold. The damp conditions that produce sprouts are also ideal for culturing mold. There are many molds that can injure or kill your bird. The key to avoiding mold is sanitation. The safest way to produce home-grown sprouts is to use clean utensils, fresh seeds, and to rinse the sprouting seeds several times a day in fresh water. Avoid growing sprouts during very hot and humid weather. You should feed them to your cockatiel as soon as possible after the green shoots appear.

Calcium

Birds need calcium in their diets. This can be provided in a number of ways. Some cockatiels will eat oyster shell, which can be purchased at a feed store. Perhaps the easiest way to provide calcium for your bird is to buy a cuttlebone that can be attached to the cage. The mantle of the cuttlefish

Good Eating

Kids Can Help at Feeding Time

Since most children enjoy activities in the kitchen, preparing food for the family pet can be the impetus for family discussions about their cockatiel's health and sustenance. Remember that the care and feeding of a bird should never be left solely up to a child. Parents should always monitor the process.

As with any meal preparation, it is important to always wash your hands before handling any food. This is also a good time for a discussion about the necessity of good hygiene, especially when handling pets.

Activities for young children ages 3 to 6:
• Fill the water bottle or dish after the parent has thoroughly cleaned it.
• Fill food dishes with pellets or seeds.

Tip: To prevent overfilling the bowls and thus making a mess in the kitchen, draw a line on the outside of the feed dish to show how full the dish should be. This will increase your child's independence and also point out the importance of portion control.

Activities for children ages 6 to 9:
• Grate carrots
• Shred lettuce

Tip: As with any cooking project, preparation makes the job easier. Get out the grater, the cutting board, and a container to hold the vegetables after they have been prepared. Show your child how to use the tools before handing over the job to him or her.

Activities for children ages 9 to 12:
• Cut fruit and vegetables (parents should always supervise children when they are using knives)
• Help make mixture for bread and for soup

The following topics are good for discussion when working in the kitchen with your child:
• Elements of a balanced diet for humans and for birds
• Importance of fresh water for birds as well as people
• Choosing healthy foods
• Portion control

Parents might also want to create a responsibility chart to help their children keep track of their jobs. Using a monthly calendar, write down your child's name and the task you have assigned him or her. Buy a pack of stickers. Only place a sticker on the calendar when you have checked to see that the job is complete and done correctly. For the younger child, you can list the steps to follow in performing the job.

To provide variety, cooked table foods, like beans, can be a stimulating addition to your bird's diet.

(cephalopod) is one of the best sources of calcium you can find. Manufactured mineral blocks are also readily obtainable at your pet store and also attach to the cage. They contain other sources of nutrition as well as calcium, and birds enjoy nibbling at them. These blocks also serve another function — keeping your bird's beak trim. It is important to always have this calcium source available.

Picky Eaters

If you think that only children can be picky eaters, think again. Some cockatiels fit this description perfectly. Your bird will let you know which foods and mixtures he likes best, but make sure not to let it get too one-sided, since a variety of foods is important. The best way to deal with a finicky bird is to never give him a chance to get choosy. In the wild, a bird eats whatever he finds, whenever he finds it. He cannot count on the same thing every morning — or even that there will be something to eat. Your cockatiel should be fed a wide variety of foods. Constantly changing the menu will help prevent your bird from becoming a picky eater. He will quickly learn to expect something different every time. In fact, most birds seem to look forward to feeding under such a schedule and enjoy finding out what's on the menu each day.

Obesity in Birds—Is There Such a Thing?

Perhaps the last thing you'd ever think of when looking at your cockatiel is that he could be overweight. While the signs are not as obvious, obesity is a serious problem among pet birds. The cause of this is the same as in humans—too much of a good thing.

Birds will generally overeat basic foods like pellets, grains, and vegetables. It is high-fat treats that cause the most problem, as well as an all-seed diet, which is not only lacking in necessary nutrients, but is also the cause of weight gain in birds.

Chapter 4

Looking Good

If you think that grooming is all about appearance, think again. Grooming is an important part of your bird's constitution. He spends a good part of his day tending to the condition of his feathers and skin. There is more than just a strong correlation between looking good and feeling good—hygiene is a necessary factor in maintaining good health and promoting longevity. Therefore, it is not only important for an owner to make sure the bird's environment is clean, but that his bird is properly groomed as well.

Often considered a special time spent between pet and owner, grooming gives you an opportunity to bond with your cockatiel. Holding him, nurturing him, and providing for his basic needs can give you an appreciation for the remarkable creature that he truly is. You literally hold his precious life in your hands. In turn, being cuddled and cared for makes your feathered pal feel secure, and it strengthens the bond of trust and affection you share.

Grooming sessions are also an ideal time to give your bird a visual examination. You can look for anything unusual in his overall appearance, such as lumps or bumps, cuts or bruises, or skin abnormalities. You can also check the condition of the feathers, beak, and nails. Regular grooming helps keep your bird healthy, but it can also aid you in spotting any potential problems early.

Bathing

Good grooming begins with keeping the body clean. Most cockatiels enjoy splashing in the water, and bath time is quite an enjoyable activity for them. This is fortunate because bathing helps to keep feathers in good condition and protects birds from getting dry skin. As mentioned earlier, you can purchase a birdbath rather inexpensively, or you can use a container you already have. A large, open glass dish set on the cage floor works well. The bath should be shallow enough that the bird can stand in it without water touching his belly. Never leave the birdbath in the cage all the time. Remove it when your cockatiel has finished splashing and dunking.

Baths should always take place in the morning so that your cockatiel will

Grooming is a normal part of your bird's daily routine. Having clean, well-maintained feathers helps your cockatiel feel his best.

Grooming=Bonding

Cockatiels love attention, and most of them enjoy being handled by their owners. In addition to play time, grooming can provide a special occasion for both bird and owner. The physical contact is beneficial in establishing a bond of trust. Grooming will also offer you an opportunity to give your pet affection and special attention. A regular grooming routine can become an anticipated treat for both of you to enjoy. Some cockatiels grow quite fond of grooming and enjoy perching on their owners' hands for some misting. Others need to be introduced to each procedure gradually. When performing the more difficult ones, such as wing clipping or nail trimming, it helps to murmur softly to your bird to reassure him. Reward your pet with treats so that he doesn't panic while you are working on these necessary chores. He may soon learn to relax and grow more comfortable with future grooming sessions.

have ample time to dry off before going to sleep at night. You want to avoid having him settle in for his evening rest with wet feathers. Do not use a blow dryer on your bird; the feathers should dry naturally.

Some owners find that setting the bath container in a sink or bathtub rather than placing it in the cage will greatly ease after-bath cleanups. If you choose to bathe your cockatiel directly in the sink, make sure that there is no residual dishwashing liquid in it as this could prove harmful to your pet. Never let your cockatiel bathe in water containing harsh cleaning agents or detergents; use only a pet shampoo that is safe for cockatiels. Also make sure that you don't fill any container or tub with too much water; an inch is sufficient. Birds can easily drown when the water is too high. If you choose to use the sink or tub for bath time fun, it will make being out of the cage more special for your pet.

Misting

Most birds enjoy being misted by their owners. A small spray bottle can be used to give your cockatiel a gentle shower. If he is reluctant when you first attempt this and seems afraid to be misted, try spraying the water below him and gradually aim higher until your cockatiel is completely comfortable with the process.

You can let your bird take a bath as often as he wants. Cockatiels should have baths several times a week and should be misted daily for optimum hygiene. During bath time or misting, it's important to keep your bird in a draft-free, warm place so he can preen himself dry. Again, make sure that your cockatiel never goes to sleep while still wet.

Nail Care

Nail trimming isn't performed simply for cosmetic reasons or to keep you from being scratched; overgrown nails can be hazardous to your bird. They can get caught in cage bars, toys, or food dishes. Along with provoking stress and fright, these situations can result in serious injuries or even death if the bird in distress is not discovered quickly. When your cockatiel's nails are too long, perching can become uncomfortable. This lack of grooming can also lead to serious foot problems.

In the wild, cockatiels keep their toenails and beaks in proper trim by engaging in their natural chewing and climbing behaviors. In captivity,

Grooming as a Health Check

Whenever you trim your bird's nails or feathers, it is an ideal time to visually and physically inspect him to check his overall appearance and health. Note the condition of the feathers. Look at your bird's body to see if there are any cuts, sores, lumps, bruises, or skin problems. Feel the keel bone (it runs vertically along the breast), and make sure that the bird isn't too thin. The keel bone should be prominent, but there should be flesh on either side of it. If it is very sharp, the bird is too thin; if you can't feel it at all, he may be too heavy or have a tumor

there. Examine the condition of the beak. Is it growing too long? Is it growing abnormally? Check the feet to see if they are in good shape.

By thoroughly examining your bird on a regular basis, you can identify potential health problems and have them treated before they become serious or even fatal. True to their wild instincts, birds can often conceal their illnesses in order not to appear vulnerable. By the time you may notice a more obvious problem, it may be too late to save your feathered friend.

however, it is sometimes difficult for a bird to stay well-trimmed. If there are insufficient opportunities to do this in a cage environment, it is up to the owner to trim the nails.

Some birds never need their nails trimmed by their owners, while others require it on a regular basis. Providing perches of different sizes can assist in the natural wear of nails. Lava rock (often sold for use in aquariums as a decoration) placed on the cage floor is also helpful. Whenever the bird perches or walks on the rock, the abrasive nature of the lava will help wear down nails. In addition, you can include a cement perch, which the bird can use to help keep his beak trimmed.

If, despite having these objects in the cage, it is still necessary to trim the nails, it is best to get instruction from your veterinarian before trying it on your own. The procedure is simple, but it can be difficult to restrain your bird

You will need to clip each nail individually with a sharp instrument. Clippers designed for human use are often more preferable; they are generally of higher quality, and they work better. When clipping the nails, make sure to cut them back to a normal length while being careful to avoid nicking the vein in the nail. If you do nick it, the nail will bleed. Use a styptic pencil or even a pinch of cornstarch to stem

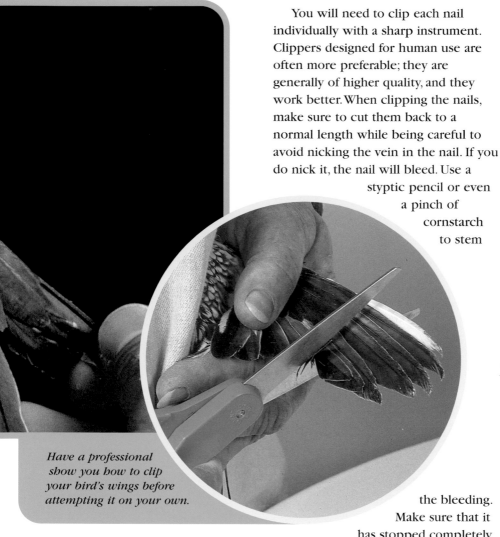

Have a professional show you how to clip your bird's wings before attempting it on your own.

the bleeding. Make sure that it has stopped completely before releasing the bird.

unless you know how to do so safely. Even the tamest cockatiel may not hold still for nail trimming. Sometimes restraining him by wrapping him loosely in a towel is helpful; this keeps him from flapping his wings and injuring himself.

You will not be able to see the nail vein in a normal gray cockatiel. In some varieties, such as the lutino, you can spot the dark red vein and thus avoid cutting it. It is best to familiarize yourself with your bird's nails before

Necessary Grooming Supplies

Bathtubs: For good looks and optimum health, your cockatiel will need to bathe regularly. You can easily purchase a birdbath at your local pet store. Some of them have a mirror on the bottom to entice your bird into staying longer in the tub. You can also use a shallow dish such as a pie pan. Always remember that a dish that is too deep and filled with more than an inch (2.5 cm) of water could be a potential safety hazard.

Nail Scissors: To keep toenails from growing too long, you will need to use a pair of sharp nail scissors. It's helpful to have styptic powder or a styptic pencil to stop bleeding should you trim the nail too closely.

Cuttlebones: As well as being a natural tool for trimming your bird's beak, a cuttlebone is a good source of calcium.

you attempt to trim them on your own, as this will help you to avoid an unpleasant grooming situation.

There is another very good reason to make sure your cockatiel's nails are kept trimmed—you. Long nails can hurt your skin! You'll feel more like handling your pet if you aren't scratched.

Beak Care

Beak trimming is far more complicated than nail trimming. Fortunately, it is rarely required since birds have access to cuttlebones, stones, and wooden perches. Because some birds have hard or fast-growing beaks, there are conditions that may require you to occasionally make adjustments. When the upper beak, or mandible, becomes extended or the shape of it is distorted, it can interfere with normal feeding. If left unattended, a bird could have difficulty eating and may actually starve to death.

Never attempt beak trimming yourself because if the mandibles do not fit together properly after the trim, your cockatiel may be worse off than before. If you feel that your bird needs his beak trimmed, consult your avian vet. This procedure is best left to an experienced professional.

Wing Clipping

It may sound like a cruel thing to do, but many avian enthusiasts clip their birds' wings as a safety measure. The

Your cockatiel's toenails should wear down naturally from normal activities like perching, but you'll have to trim them if they grow too long.

breeder perform this procedure before you try it.

Feather Facts

Before you begin clipping, you should know a little about your bird's feathers. Cockatiels have several types of feathers. Each serves a different purpose. The longest ones are the primary flight feathers; they give the bird lift when he flaps his wings.

The secondary flight feathers provide air resistance and protect a bird from just dropping to the ground; they allow him to gradually float to the floor.

Clipping Procedure

It is easiest to clip a bird's wings if you have the help of an assistant. He or she can hold the bird belly up in a secure position, and then stretch out one wing at a time, holding it still as you clip it. In this position, it's easier to see the

procedure simply consists of trimming the tips of the flight feathers. Wing clipping is the equivalent of getting a haircut. Just as a trim doesn't hurt you at all, the same is true of clipping your bird's wings. Your cockatiel will still achieve enough lift with clipped wings to be able to flutter to the ground. You might want to watch a veterinarian or

Overgrown Beaks

Never attempt to trim your bird's beak yourself. An avian veterinarian should examine and treat any excessive or abnormal growth. Although most beaks stay trimmed with a bird's natural chewing behaviors, one that becomes overgrown may also indicate an underlying medical problem that should be diagnosed.

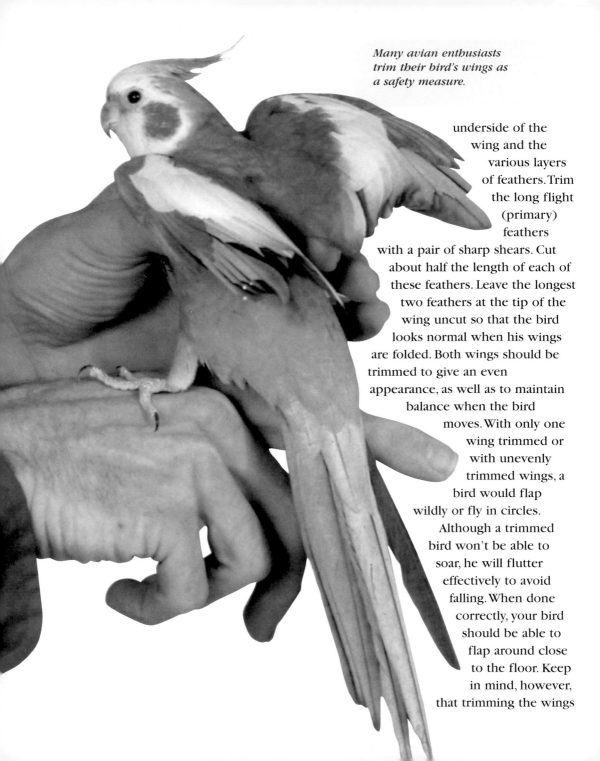

underside of the wing and the various layers of feathers. Trim the long flight (primary) feathers with a pair of sharp shears. Cut about half the length of each of these feathers. Leave the longest two feathers at the tip of the wing uncut so that the bird looks normal when his wings are folded. Both wings should be trimmed to give an even appearance, as well as to maintain balance when the bird moves. With only one wing trimmed or with unevenly trimmed wings, a bird would flap wildly or fly in circles. Although a trimmed bird won't be able to soar, he will flutter effectively to avoid falling. When done correctly, your bird should be able to flap around close to the floor. Keep in mind, however, that trimming the wings

Molting

Molting is the natural process by which a bird's old and tattered feathers are gradually replaced with new ones. A bird will shed his feathers in a short period of time and grow new ones. Most birds molt once a year, usually in the summer.

While some cockatiels will have a scruffy appearance during molting, the process is not often noticeable to most bird owners. You should not see any bald patches. If you notice unusual looking feathers, have your bird checked immediately by an avian vet. Don't be concerned if you find feathers in the cage at other times of the year. Cockatiels are always losing a few. Once you have witnessed a molt, you will never again be fooled by regular feather loss. While molting isn't painful, some cockatiels may experience itching. You may also notice some behavioral changes. Your bird might not want as much attention as usual.

Additionally, a single cockatiel doesn't have another bird to help him at molting time to remove feather sheathes on his head and face. All he can do it scratch at them. You can help with this process. If your bird is very tame, have him sit on your shoulder or chest while you gently rub the sheathes between the fingernails of your thumb and forefinger. Not only does this feel good to the bird, it's nice bonding time. If he quarrels or gets agitated, just be gentler with your touch.

During the molt, and just prior to it, it is a good idea to provide your bird with extra protein. Eggs, along with fresh vegetables for vitamins, will help your bird stay healthy during this stressful time.

will also take away you pet's ability to fly away from danger. If you have other pets in your household, make sure that they are safely out of the way whenever your bird is outside of his cage.

To Clip or Not to Clip

There are several schools of thought on the subject of wing clipping. Some people feel that it is best to perform the procedure in order to keep birds in captivity from escaping and getting lost or hurt in unfamiliar environments. To add to the argument, there are a few indoor hazards your bird could face if you leave him untrimmed. For example, unclipped birds can fly into mirrors or glass doors. They can also fly onto hot stoves, get caught in ceiling fans, or become trapped in cabinets or closets.

The opposing school of thought is that all birds need to learn how to fly, and until they have mastered flight, they need full feathers. Some believe that when you clip a bird's wings, you deprive him of the marvelous miracle of flight to which he has been endowed—birds should be allowed their natural behaviors and their freedom.

The bottom line is that flying is a necessary form of exercise for all cockatiels. Therefore, if you keep your cockatiel's wings trimmed, you should make sure that he has plenty of other options for physical activity—inside

and outside the cage. Toys are important furnishings in every enclosure. Likewise, a play gym is an excellent way to provide your cockatiel with a workout and mental stimulation during out-of-cage time. Good workout toys include ladders, swings, and perches your bird will love to climb.

In any case, whether you subscribe to clipping the wings or not, it is imperative that you take precautions whenever your bird is out and about.

FAMILY-FRIENDLY TIP

Can a Child Help with Grooming?

Although the more difficult grooming procedures should be left to adults, that doesn't mean a child can't take some part in these pet care responsibilities. Your youngster can participate by gathering the tools and supplies needed for the grooming chore at hand. He or she can watch while you are physically inspecting the bird. You can explain what you are doing and discuss the importance of grooming for the cockatiel's health. The more you include your child in the care process, the more he will learn about his pet and become bonded to him.

How Much to Clip

Some owners decide to trim the lower half of their bird's primary flight feathers to prevent them from flying. It's important to keep in mind that clipping should allow your parakeet to flutter gently to the floor. If you cut too much, there is potential for injury from falling. If you cut too little your bird could fly off into the wild blue yonder. Therefore, it's best to have someone experienced like an avian veterinarian or breeder do it for you or teach you how to do it properly.

Some birds are such strong fliers that, even with their wings clipped, they are still able to escape through an open window or fly away when outdoors. For safety's sake, never take your cockatiel outside unless he is in an escape-proof cage or carrier. Escape-proof means that the doors and latches are wired shut or padlocked—birds are very adept at picking simple locks!

Another word of caution: Some of the little travel cages available in retail stores are flimsy and can come apart quite easily. Although they are secure enough when placed on a table, the bottoms are apt to come loose when they are carried around. Make sure all enclosures are sturdy and in good condition before taking your bird outdoors.

Chapter 5

Feeling Good

When it comes to protecting your health, you look for a doctor that will meet your physical needs, as well as someone you trust and relate to who can give you sound advice. If you have a problem, you want to be sure that your doctor will be able to give you the latest information for the best possible care.

W hen choosing a veterinarian for your bird, you should use the same criteria. Just as you wouldn't think to go to a cardiologist for a broken arm, you shouldn't expect all vets to have the specialized knowledge needed to care for your cockatiel. For basic avian health care, a general practitioner can give your bird the attention and care he needs. However, it would serve you well to find a vet who specializes in practicing avian medicine.

Finding a Good Avian Vet

The best time to find a good veterinarian is before you need one. When your pet is in distress, you don't have the time to check out a vet's references or make inquiries into his area of expertise. Likewise, in an emergency, you don't have time to find the location of your nearest bird hospital. Cockatiels, as well as many other birds, often mask symptoms of illness. By the time it is evident that there is something wrong, the situation is critical. Therefore, having a vet you can turn to at such times is vital for the long life of your pet.

To maintain good health, your cockatiel should receive a well-bird checkup from an avian veterinarian at least once a year.

When seeking an avian vet, you will want to find a doctor who will answer your questions, give you advice, and be available in cases of emergency.

Look for a Specialist

A terrific way of finding a qualified vet is through referral. If you ask anyone you know who keeps birds to recommend a vet, they'll give you their honest opinions of why they use a certain doctor. Ask specific question to get a feel for the vet's personality and the type of practice he has. After getting several recommendations, contact these doctors and make an appointment to meet each one and visit the office.

It stands to reason that your main

criterion when choosing a vet is that he has the knowledge needed to treat your pet. While any vet has training to treat birds, there are some who choose to make this a specialty. Many of these doctors have had significant experience and regularly study the latest scientific information. They often belong to the Association of Avian Veterinarians.

Only Part of the Picture

Choosing a specialist is only part of the picture. There are a number of other elements you should look for when selecting your pet's doctor. When taking your bird to the vet, you want to go to an office that is well organized and where the technicians and office staff are professional. It's not enough to have a competent vet if the rest of the staff is untrained, and the office is poorly run. You'll know you are in the right place because it will be apparent that they love animals and enjoy working with them. Also, cleanliness is an essential ingredient for a good veterinary practice; the waiting rooms and examining rooms should be clean and comfortable.

You'll want to ask some questions. Ask how many vets are in the practice, what services are offered, what the fees are, and what hours the office is open. Since there is never a convenient time for an emergency, you'll want to know what provisions they offer for handling these situations. It's particularly

Choosing the Right Vet

Ideally, you should select a veterinarian for your new cockatiel before bringing him home. When looking for an avian specialist, keep these 4 Cs in mind:

Credentials: Ask what training the doctor has in avian medicine.

Convenience: Assuming that the location is convenient, ask what the business hours are and how emergencies are handled.

Care: If asking a friend about a vet, also ask about the technicians and office staff. A caring staff is essential for proper care.

Communication: Ask how appointments are scheduled and what follow-up is practiced. Many vets call several days after an appointment to check on the bird to see how he's doing with treatment. An efficient office will maintain excellent communication between the doctor and the patient's family.

Arrange to take your new cockatiel to the vet for a complete physical examination a few days after bringing him home to ensure he is in good condition.

important to know the proper procedure for emergencies well in advance.

Another deciding factor is the location of the veterinary office. You'll want to keep convenience in mind for you and your pet. It is often traumatic taking an animal for a veterinary visit. If it is a far distance, your bird might become agitated during the trip.

Meet and Greet

Once you've found a specialist with convenient hours in close proximity, you'll want to schedule a visit to get to know him or her. You'll want to know the staff at the vet's office, and they'll want to know you. It's a great time to ask questions such as how frequently you should take your bird for a checkup. Go over any concerns you have about caring for your pet. Ask for a tour of the facilities. Remember, you are establishing a relationship centered on your pet's well-being.

The First Vet Visit

Your first visit to the vet with your cockatiel will be filled with pride. You'll be excited to show off your new pet. Your vet will be able to give you information about feeding, grooming, and other essential care. This visit is important in order for the doctor to establish some base-line measurements. For example, he or she will want to know how much your cockatiel weighs. In the future, the doctor can begin to determine if there is a problem by checking to see if your pet has lost weight. But just what should you expect when you take your new cockatiel for his first checkup? You can

FAMILY-FRIENDLY TIP

Your Child's First Vet Visit

Before your child accompanies you to the vet's office for your cockatiel's checkup, discuss each part of the exam—medical history, physical observation, and hands-on exam—with him or her prior to the appointment. Explain that, although the bird might flutter, squirm, and try to get away, the doctor isn't hurting him.

Most children are keen observers. Talk to your child about the importance of noticing changes in your pet and the significance of any unusual signs in his appearance or behavior. Explain that, in this way, he or she is contributing to the pet's care because the earlier you spot a difficulty, the more likely your vet will be able to treat it.

expect the procedure to be conducted professionally and pretty much like your first medical exam.

The vet will be interested in your cockatiel's history. You'll be asked to discuss your bird's background. You'll have an opportunity to explain where you got your bird and as much information as you know about the

seller. The vet will also want to know how long you've had your pet and details about how you are caring for him. It's important to tell the doctor about the bird's new environment, such as if there are other birds or pets in the household. This is the perfect time to get into discussions about what you are feeding your cockatiel, how much exercise he needs, and how to meet his grooming needs.

The Physical Exam

The next part of the visit is the physical examination. The doctor will give your cockatiel a thorough checkup from the tip of his beautiful crest to the bottom of his feet. He or she will want to observe your bird for a few minutes to inspect the overall appearance of your pet: the general condition of the body, skin, feet, feathers, eyes, ears, and vent. The vet will also look at your bird's posture and watch to see if there are any signs of respiratory difficulties.

After observation, the vet will perform a hands-on exam to check the condition of the feathers, the feel of the muscle tone, and to get a closer look at the eyes, ears, beak, etc. He or she will weigh your bird in grams, which is a better method for determining weight in small increments.

If need be, the vet will order tests, such as the chlamydophila test for parrot fever. He or she might check the

Feeling Good

droppings to detect any visible signs of health problems or diseases.

If all goes well, you'll be asked to make a yearly visit to promote your cockatiel's optimum good health.

Don't hesitate to ask your vet to explain things during the exam. It is important to learn as much about your pet as you can. Vets would rather have you ask questions than jeopardize your pet's health due to ignorance.

Spotting Health Problems

Nobody knows your cockatiel like you do. You'll learn to watch for subtle changes in physical appearance or changes in behavior that indicate something is wrong with him. Your vet will depend on your keen observations to help diagnose problems. Playing with and caring for your pet on a daily basis will give you an idea of what's normal for him. Even though you'll know what's usual for your bird and when behavior or appearance change, it's nice to have some specific guidelines that help you recognize when something is wrong.

Tell-Tale Signs of Illness

If your cockatiel is listless and doesn't show interest in the usual activities, this could be an indication that something is wrong. Check to see if your bird sits at the bottom of his cage or on a perch and appears to have a general lack of energy. Lack of appetite is another sign that your bird isn't feeling well. If he shows any changes in his normal routine—sleeping, eating, and playing with toys—take notice. These indicators let you know that something is amiss

Only an avian specialist should diagnose and treat any health problems your bird may have.

Health Alert

A healthy cockatiel is usually active, vocal, and keeps his feathers in good condition. An ill cockatiel may not keep up with grooming and "let himself go." He may also look sleepy and listless and spend a lot of time on the bottom of the cage. If you notice anything unusual over an extended period, seek veterinary attention promptly because a bird's condition can decline rapidly.

and that you need to schedule an appointment with your vet.

Your cockatiel might start exhibiting some behaviors that you haven't noticed before. Check with your doctor if you see that your bird is having difficulty standing, walking, or is sleeping all of the time, drinking or eating more than usual, has a drooping head, wings, or tail, engages in excessive feather plucking, or is vomiting.

If your cockatiel has an untidy appearance or if the vent is soiled, this could also be a signal that something is not right. Check to see the condition of the feathers or if there is abnormal feather growth. Look for swelling around the eyes, nasal or eye discharges, and abnormal droppings. Take note if you see any lumps or swellings. Notice your bird's posture. If he is hunched over, this indicates a concern. Of course, should you see bleeding, there is an obvious and serious problem.

Sometimes your first sign of difficulty will be the sound of wheezing, clicking, or raspy vocalizations that indicate that there might be some respiratory distress. If your pet is coughing, sneezing, or has labored breathing, you should seek medical advice immediately.

Your conclusions can mean the difference between life and death. While some signs are more serious than others, it is best to discuss all observations with your pet health care provider. A sick bird should always be considered a medical emergency, and you should seek help immediately. Never try to treat your bird yourself. Over-the-counter remedies can make the situation worse. Again, keep in mind that birds are good at masking illness. By the time you notice that there is a problem, it is usually serious.

Reproductive Problems

Occasionally, an unpaired hen will produce an egg. Controlled by

Feeling Good

Signs and Symptoms: What They Mean

As a responsible bird owner, it is critical to recognize signs of illness in your cockatiel. The following changes in your bird's behavior or appearance could signal the onset of a problem that may require a trip to the vet:

Fluffiness: If your cockatiel has his feathers fluffed, he is trying to keep heat close to his skin and is having trouble regulating his temperature. Fluffiness might occur with sleepiness, sleeping on two feet instead of one, or sleeping on the bottom of the cage.

Sleeping too much: A sick bird may sleep more than usual. Sleeping on the bottom of the cage or sleeping on two feet is also telling.

Loss of appetite: You should know how much and what your cockatiel is consuming each day. If you notice that your bird is not eating enough or if he stops eating, there is a problem.

Attitude change: Your cockatiel might be ill if he seems listless and is not behaving in his usual manner.

Lameness: If your bird can't use his feet, you can be guaranteed that there is a problem. Lameness can occur as a result of egg binding, injury, seizure, or other conditions.

Panting or labored breathing: Either of these symptoms can indicate a respiratory ailment, or perhaps overheating.

hormones, sometimes a bird in top condition may be so stimulated to reproduce that she will lay eggs even in the absence of a mate. Some birds will burrow under newspaper or in a cavity around the house and create a nest, while others will lay an egg on the bare floor. It is not always easy to stop them. If the female produces more than a few eggs and you leave them in the cage, she may settle in and incubate a clutch of infertile eggs. This means she will do nothing but sit on them for a few weeks, a behavior that is potentially hazardous. A cockatiel is not a chicken and is therefore not equipped to produce an unending string of eggs. Her adaptations and instincts cause her to produce until she has accumulated enough to incubate, but if that is short-circuited by your

removal of the eggs, she might continue to lay a large number of them. It is very important that you take your cockatiel to the doctor.

Sometimes a bird can be egg bound, which means that the female has difficulty expelling the egg from her body. This can be caused by a deformity in the egg, or it can be a result of a diet lacking in proper nutrition. Obesity, lack of exercise, and a poor environment can also cause this condition.

Egg binding is very serious and can be fatal. If you notice that your female cockatiel is on the bottom of the cage and appears to be straining, it could indicate this serious condition. With emergency medical treatment, it is possible to release the egg. The key to treating egg binding is to get your bird to the doctor as soon as you notice any symptoms. If left untreated, your bird will go into shock. She has the best chance of survival if the condition is treated immediately.

Specific Avian Illnesses

Chlamydia/Psittacosis
With the advances of research in avian medicine, much has been learned

81

Feeling Good

Emergencies: How to Know

How can you tell if your cockatiel is in distress and needs urgent medical care? The following symptoms are signs of a severe medical condition that will require immediate veterinary care. If your bird exhibits any of these symptoms, contact your vet immediately and seek medical treatment:

- bleeding
- diarrhea
- difficulty breathing
- inability to stand or walk
- seizures
- vomiting

about chlamydia/psittacosis, also known as parrot fever, and how to diagnose and treat it.

Symptoms: Your cockatiel will be lethargic and the feathers will appear fluffed up. He will have difficulty breathing, with symptoms of sinusitis or conjunctivitis. Look for yellowish to greenish droppings. Your doctor will be able to determine if your cockatiel has lost weight. He can become dehydrated, and this can lead to death if treatment isn't given immediately.

Treatment: There is a screening test that your vet will probably use as a part of your new bird exam, as well as his annual checkup. If it is determined

that your cockatiel is suffering from this disease, the doctor will prescribe a medication that will be administered by weekly injections or in water. The treatment lasts for 45 days.

Giardia/ Intestinal Motile Protozoa

Giardia is a parasitic disease commonly found in birds. This one-celled organism lives in the small intestine and is shed sporadically in the bird's droppings.

Symptoms: Look for diarrhea, itching, and flaky skin for this often difficult-to-diagnose disease. The bird's droppings often have an unusually bad odor. In adults, the itching will cause the bird to scream and pull out his feathers. In babies, the birds seem to be thin, will scream excessively, and have poor-looking feathers.

Treatment: Since the organism isn't shed in every dropping, this disease is often difficult to diagnose right away. In the past, treatment consisted of injections, which are not good for the bird, or a very bitter tasting pill that was hard to get the bird to ingest. Now there are new medicines that can be administered easily in your pet's drinking water for seven days.

While this won't guarantee your pet won't contract giardia, the use of water bottles instead of a water dish can certainly be a big step in preventing it. Not using a dish will prevent contamination of the drinking water with fecal material. This disease is

An Unplanned Pregnancy

Breeding is a decision that shouldn't be made lightly. If you decide that you want to breed your cockatiel, you'll need to make a commitment of extra time, energy, and expense. You will have to devote lots of time to the care and feeding of the new baby birds. You will also want to make sure your female is a good candidate for breeding and in good condition to endure this process. But if you decide this is not for you, congratulate yourself on making a responsible decision.

But what if the unthinkable happens? What if your birds mate, and the female produces eggs? It's not the end of the world. Cockatiels breed throughout the year, and this can easily happen. Unwanted eggs should be removed from the cage, however. After disposing of the eggs, check to make sure that the bird isn't continuing to lay more. This could prove to be hazardous to her health. If the egg laying continues, you might want to consult your vet for further advice.

controllable, but it is often difficult to cure. Your pet may have outbreaks periodically, so watch for the symptoms. If you detect even one of them, contact your vet immediately.

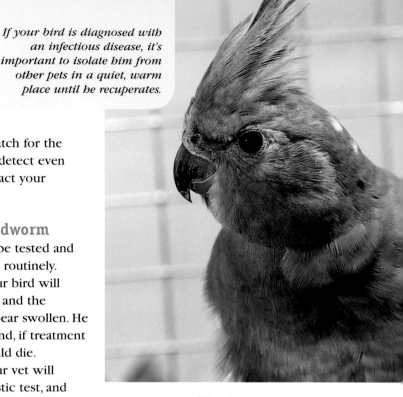

If your bird is diagnosed with an infectious disease, it's important to isolate him from other pets in a quiet, warm place until he recuperates.

Ascarids/Roundworm

Your bird should be tested and treated for worms routinely.

Symptoms: Your bird will appear fluffed up, and the abdomen will appear swollen. He will lose weight and, if treatment isn't given, he could die.

Treatment: Your vet will perform a diagnostic test, and then treat the condition with medication.

Candida

Candida, or yeast infection as it is commonly known, can present a number of problems in your cockatiel. Secondary infections often appear.

Symptoms: Visually, your pet will appear to be sick. He will huddle and be reluctant to move. There can be weight loss while appetite increases.

Treatment: Your vet might use a combination of drugs to treat candida. The medicine is given once or twice a day for at least five days.

Aspergillosis

This avian disease is a fungal infection caused by spores that grow in damp, unclean conditions.

Symptoms: Your cockatiel will have trouble breathing and will be extremely lethargic. It is essential to get him help immediately.

Treatment: This infection is often hard to diagnose because the symptoms are the same for a number of other avian diseases. The vet will rule out other possible causes for the symptoms exhibited by examining and testing your bird. Once aspergillosis is diagnosed, the vet will treat it systemically by giving medicine that will spread throughout the entire body if

indicated. If the problem seems localized, your vet will use medications to treat the infected area.

Mites

The most common parasite of birds is mites. Tiny arthropods that are barely visible to the eye, some mites live on the actual host, while others live elsewhere but still attack the bird. If you know what to look for, mites can be spotted by gently separating your cockatiel's feathers. Look for a small white, tan, or red moving speck. While it isn't always possible to spot mites, you'll have better luck trying to detect them at night. Leave a white paper towel or piece of paper on the bottom of the cage. Check in about an hour for

Stress

If you've ever thought about trading places with your cockatiel after a stressful day at work, you might reconsider when you learn that your cockatiel can also suffer from stress. There are several types of stress in a bird—disease related, behavioral, or environmental. If your pet is suffering from an illness, your vet will be able to give him medication that will alleviate the symptoms of stress while curing the physical or mental problem. If the problem is related to environmental or behavior issues, there are a number of things you can do to make life easier for your bird. Make sure your pet has a balanced diet, and gets plenty of sleep, exercise, and bonding time with you.

The best way to protect your cockatiel from ill health is to simply offer him clean, dry living conditions and a healthy, loving environment.

red specks on the paper. Other mites may appear as crusty skin.

Symptoms: Some mites are easy to spot, such as the red mite that literally can be seen as tiny specks of red. Birds become nervous and pick at themselves. Other mites are not visible to the naked eye, and your bird will depend on your keen observation for tell-tale signs. Look for crusty skin on the cere, vent, or feet.

Treatment: The doctor may prescribe an oral medication, as well as a topical ointment. But remember, with parasites you must treat the bird's environment as well as the bird. The entire cage should be thoroughly cleaned.

Heavy Metal Poisoning

You already know that cages should be made of stainless steel that is powder-baked or polymer-covered, so your bird will be safe from metal poisoning. Not so fast! If you think that the danger of metal poisoning comes only from cages made of lead, zinc, brass, tin, or copper, think again. There are dangers lurking in other areas as well. Look out for rusty metal, lead, and copper wiring. If you think that your bird isn't exposed to any of these dangers, be warned they can be found by your cockatiel in costume jewelry, metal toys, and lead-based paint.

Quarantine

A new addition is great fun for a family, but you can run the risk of spreading disease to your bird when you add other pets to the household. Before you add another bird to the cage, it is recommended that you quarantine him until your vet pronounces him in good health and free from transmittable disease.

Also, it's fun to get together with other bird lovers at pet fairs and shows. This, too, can be the cause of spreading disease. Infections can spread even if you are diligent and don't allow direct contact. Diseases can be airborne or spread through the failure of humans to wash their hands frequently after handling animals, equipment, etc.

Obesity

Obesity is a health risk at any age, but in the later stages of your pet's life, it can cause liver and pancreas problems. Just as with humans, it is the result of taking in more calories than are burned. In the wild, birds have more opportunity for an active lifestyle. In captivity, birds should have several hours outside the cage for exercise. If they have a diet composed of mostly seeds, they are more prone to becoming obese.

The remedy for obesity is the same as that for humans: Stop buying snack foods, and start serving more fruits and vegetables. To counteract weight gain, refrain from giving your bird an all-seed diet. If your bird seems to be eating seeds and refuses to stop, only leave the seeds in the cage for ten minutes in the morning and again for ten minutes at night. Have fruits and vegetables available at all other times.

Senior Bird Care

As your pet ages, you must continue to make sure that you provide exercise on a daily basis. While his activity level may decrease and he may require more sleep than before, this doesn't mean that you should neglect his need for physical and mental stimulation. Your cockatiel still needs time outside the cage. He will still want and need the companionship that you have provided over the years.

You might need to adjust the food you give your senior cockatiel. Check with the vet to see if your bird is getting all of the vitamins and nutrients that are needed during these senior years. Your vet might recommend cutting back on the amount of food due to decreased activity.

Chapter 6

Being Good

Have you ever felt like you were being held captive by your pet or your kids? It's not a good feeling. If you've occasionally thought that you were performing certain tasks just to avoid an unpleasant scene, face it — you are not in control. The answer, of course, is training. If you want to have an enjoyable life with your cockatiel, or any other pet, then it's almost mandatory that you establish some basic rules of discipline that will let your pet know what is expected of him.

Basic training is simply that—discipline. Sticking to a general code of behavior helps everyone get along and makes life easier. The same is true of pets in the household; they need rules and boundaries, too.

Most bird behavior is motivated by instinct — avoiding pain and seeking pleasure. We often try to interpret behaviors in human terms. For example, if we come home after being away for a long time and find that our bird has scattered his food out of the dish and onto the floor, we should not assume that this action was to punish us for being away. The bird simply was acting on instinct and trying to get a certain morsel of food from the dish. Keeping their motivation in mind, coupled with your own expectations, it's easy to see that the best way to convey the message that certain rules should be followed is to establish a loving, trusting relationship before teaching the rules.

Building Trust

If thoughts of training your cockatiel to perform acrobatic feats on command in front of an enthralled audience of neighbors and friends flash through your mind, you might want to reflect on the basics of training a pet. Like all relationships, a firm foundation of trust must be established if you are ever to

Aside from allowing you to handle and protect your cockatiel, training can strengthen the bond between you and your pet.

Birdie Language

Just as you can read a person's body language by the look on his face or the way he holds his arms, your cockatiel will give you visual clues as to what he's thinking or feeling. If your cockatiel is assuming a stiff posture or if he is running away, this is his way of telling you that he is frightened or stressed. If you are reaching into the cage and observe this body language, it is best to stop what you are doing. If your cockatiel starts fanning his tail, that means that you should back off. When your pet stretches his neck and raises a foot, beware. He is telling you to go away. Flared wings or fluffed head feathers are signs that are meant to warn you that the bird is not happy. Perhaps the biggest clue that a bird is afraid is when he bites. Clearly your bird is giving you a message. On the other hand, when you are petting your cockatiel, he may bow his head and close his eyes—this is a signal that he is enjoying being petted.

accomplish anything. Without this basic element, your pet won't have the self-confidence to try the simplest of tricks. Building trust can be accomplished by having realistic goals, using positive reinforcement, and being consistent.

Realistic Goals—Fitting Tasks to Natural Behaviors

An important facet of training your cockatiel is choosing tricks or behaviors that are natural to your bird. For example, training your bird to fly through a hoop involves merely getting him to understand what you want him to do. Flying isn't contrary to your pet's nature, so you are not asking your bird to perform a task that goes against his natural instincts.

Positive Reinforcement—The Most Important Tool

When teaching the basic rules, there are two requirements: patience and rewards. Notice that punishment is not listed here. Obviously, when you are training a bird, punishment is out of the question. You can hardly give your bird "time out" or take away his allowance. What you can do is reward your pet for following the rules. Of course, this is not an easy task, but it is an attainable one. With gentle patience you can train you cockatiel to stay away from certain things such as the stove. This doesn't mean that once you've taught your pet something, you can relax and not monitor the situation. It just means that you'll have an easier time supervising your bird.

Hand-taming is a gradual process, so be patient, gentle, and practice in a quiet place where there are no distractions.

Treats as Motivational Tools

When training your cockatiel, you'll find that rewarding good behavior with a tasty treat will motivate him to repeat the behavior you want. Sunflower seeds make great treats because birds love them. However, they are high in fat, so they should be given sparingly. Your pet will let you know what other foods are special favorites.

Patience is essential in any teaching or training task. Ask any school teacher or parent, for that matter, how often they needed to remind their children after a rule had been established. You can bet that it wasn't just once. So be prepared for lots of repetition. While cockatiels are quite intelligent, keep in mind that birds are harder to teach than humans.

Throughout your training sessions, give positive reinforcement for a job well done. This can be in the form of kind words and facial expressions as well as treats. Birds will react to all of those. You might want to reserve the food treats for special rewards since obesity can be an issue with birds.

Consistency— The Key to Repeat Performance

Being consistent is essential if you want to be an effective trainer. It is very important that you are unfailing in always associating the same responses to your bird's actions. You will never be able to train your pet if you change your mind about what you want.

Training will require a game plan on your part. You should give serious thought to what you expect and how you want to reward the behavior. Then, each time you give the command and it is followed, repeat the same sounds or words, and give the treat. Gradually, the bird will come to the realization that a certain behavior will be rewarded.

Housetraining—It's Not What You Think

Probably, the first training you'll do is housetraining. Don't get excited and think that you can prevent you bird from having accidents in the house. While it is probably possible to housetrain a larger bird like a parrot, it would take a lot of time and energy. You wouldn't be successful with a cockatiel. In this context,

Pet-Proofing

If you don't want to spend hours crying about a lost pet, take that important first step: Prevent your cockatiel from getting lost. To do this, you must make your house escape-proof. Cockatiels can be little flying Harry Houdini's, discovering spots you'd never expect. Therefore, it's important to pet-proof any area to which your pet will have access. First, check that all windows and doors are closed. Even a small opening can be a potential escape hatch. Whenever your bird is out of his cage, supervise him. When you are cleaning the cage, make sure the room is sealed off by shutting the door to other areas. Just because you've clipped the

wings, that's no guarantee that your bird won't be able to fly away. When you travel with your bird, keep him in the travel cage until you have pet-proofed any areas your bird will be out of his enclosure.

If the unthinkable happens and your bird escapes, contact your neighbors to be on the lookout for your pet. Some people have their birds microchipped. Your vet can perform this simple procedure, which involves implanting a microchip containing pertinent information underneath the skin. If someone finds your bird and takes it to a vet's office, a scanner can retrieve the name and phone number of the owner.

housetraining refers to rules that you want your bird to obey when he is out of the cage. Think of it as setting limits. For example, some people do not want their cockatiel on the dinner table during mealtime. With time and patience, it is possible

to teach your pet not to do it. Cockatiels are very intelligent creatures. They will notice when you are upset. They will also notice expressions of delight and approval. Since birds are flock animals and they care about how other members of the flock feel, your cockatiel will not intentionally try to do things to displease you. In fact, in all animal training, displays of affection, time out for play, and just generally making a fuss over the animal are often more effective rewards than tidbits of favorite foods. This is not to say that treats aren't effective, but that positive reinforcement has an enormous effect .

Handling Commands

In addition to housetraining, you should teach your cockatiel a few basic commands, both for his safety and your convenience. You'll want to teach your cockatiel how to step-up on your finger. Other useful on-command behaviors might be teaching your bird to return to his cage or to lie down on your hand.

Vocal Cues

Cockatiels give vocal cues as a way of communicating with us.

- A purring noise indicates contentment.

- A growling noise indicates aggression.

- Tongue clicking is a friendly noise, perhaps an invitation to play.

- Beak clicking means your cockatiel is defending his turf.

"No"—The Most Important Command of All

The most important command for animals or children is "no." It should be one of the first rules you teach your pet. This protective act should be used if you ever spot your bird heading toward trouble. It can save his life.

Setting limitations is a way to make your pet feel secure. When the entire house is available to your bird, you'll have your hands full trying to supervise him. Your cockatiel should always be monitored when he is out of the cage. If you limit the amount of space as well as set boundaries as to appropriate areas of the room, you'll make your job easier, and your pet will feel better as well.

Step-Up and Stick Training

Begin training with the step-up command. You'll need this important command to take your cockatiel in and out of the cage, as well in many other situations. To get ready to teach your bird, begin with a confident smile on your face. Birds read our body language just as much as we

The most important behavior you can teach your bird is the step-up command.

Clicker Training

Clicker training is a fast, easy, humane way to train animals. Not only do birds love it, it actually works! Using a small plastic device that makes a clicking noise, you will employ a sound to elicit the behavior you want from your pet. You should determine what motivates your bird. Is it food or is it physical contact such as head scratching? Once you have determined what the reward is, you can then teach your bird to associate the clicking sound with the reward. When the bird hears the clicking sound, he will associate the noise with the reward that he anticipates.

Training sessions should be kept short, but they should be conducted on a regular basis. It's better to have frequent, short, consistent sessions than a long one periodically. Use a table top or counter for training. Make sure that the space is small so that the bird will concentrate and not become distracted. Most important, training should be fun and not a burden. You'll be more patient and get better results if you're both having fun.

pet. Avoid quick, sudden motions as they could frighten your bird. Gently press your extended index finger to the bird's lower abdomen. It is a natural instinct for your bird to then step-up on your finger. As the bird begins to move, say in a pleasing tone, "step-up." Wait a second, and then praise your cockatiel for a job well done.

Once your bird understands the step-up command, it is relatively easy to transfer that knowledge to stepping up on a T-stick. You can purchase these sticks at any pet store. The long handle is ideal for moving the bird in and out of the cage or for basic training. Follow the same procedures, and within a short period of time, your bird should be able to hop up on the perch or rod that you are holding.

Tricks

Now that you've taught the basic commands, just what other tricks can you teach your cockatiel? Cockatiels are mimics, so they can be trained to whistle a tune or say a few words. They can even be impersonators, barking like the family dog. You can train your cockatiel to nod "yes" and "no." You can teach your pet to pick up a toy, roll a ball, climb on your shoulder, or place a toy in a basket. If you have the time and the patience, you can train your cockatiel to do all sorts of tricks.

Talking

If you buy a cockatiel, most likely you'll

Kissing Concerns

A pop singing group once had a hit tune many years back about what happens when you kiss a guy. The answer is "enough germs to cause pneumonia." All in jest, this song was about the problems of falling in love. While showing your cockatiel some affection by giving him a "peck" generally doesn't pose any risk, there could be some potential hazards to him if you are sick. Humans can transmit bacteria to their birds through kissing. Avoid kissing your cockatiel if you have a cold, cough, cold sores, or aren't feeling well in general.

read theirs. You are setting the tone of this training session by exuding a positive attitude.

Remember to be patient and consistent. It should only take a couple of sessions for your bird to master this simple command. For more advanced training, break the activity up into small steps. Teach one step at a time.

Slowly extend your hand to your

want to teach him to talk. Cockatiels are not as adept at speaking as some other species, but they can be taught to say a few words. Because they are vocal and social animals, they will naturally pay attention to their owner's speech. Their voices tend to be high pitched and scratchy, but they are able to imitate whistles and can even imitate long tunes with a great degree of accuracy.

Keep in mind that your goal is to teach your bird to learn a few words or phrases. Pick a word, such as the bird's name or your name, or a simple phrase, such as "How are you?" Start by getting the bird's attention with a tidbit of food. Repeat the phrase over and over again. If the bird makes any sound that approximates your word or phrase, reward him by cooing an encouragement and perhaps even giving him a nibble of food. As time goes on, you can be more exacting about his performance before rewarding him.

Cockatiels will often spontaneously repeat a word or phrase that is spoken to them at a time when you are not actively trying to teach them. Once again, give them encouragement. Remember to keep your expectations realistic. Also, if your pet fails to learn to repeat a word or phrase, keep in mind that he is still a wonderful companion.

Socialization

The decision to get a cockatiel should involve all the members of your household. By bringing a pet into the home, you have made the decision to

Repetition is the key to teaching your cockatiel to talk or do tricks.

FAMILY-FRIENDLY TIP

Involving a Child in Training

Your children will love the fact that your cockatiel can do tricks. Youngsters can help train the cockatiel to talk. Have them repeat a word over and over again. Each time the bird responds appropriately, have them reward the pet with encouraging words rather than treats, as they might unintentionally frighten the bird and get bitten. Tiny tots should not be allowed to put their hands in the cage. Older children can help teach the step-up command on their fingers or on a perch. They can also feed the bird treats.

How can you determine when your child is ready for more responsibility? There isn't a magic number letting you know what age is appropriate to teach tricks or to care for a pet. As a parent, you will know when your child has the patience as well as deliberateness to work with a bird.

make him a part of your family. As such, your bird should be caged in an area where he can have a part in family life.

Whenever a new pet is introduced into the household, make sure that it is a comfortable process for all parties. If you have other pets, it is important to maintain the same amount of time and attention to these companions. It is also vital to make sure that the other animals do not have access to your new bird's cage. Accidents can happen in the blink of an eye.

You should always quarantine a new bird for a recommended period of time

Always supervise children while they are handling birds; they must be taught to hold a bird correctly and with composure.

before caging him with another feathered friend. This is for the health and safety of both birds. Your new bird could have an illness or parasite that could cause the other one to get sick. Check with your vet during your first well-bird visit to see when you can house them together.

Young children are as curious about new pets as the pets are about them. Establish some guidelines for the bird's safety as well as that of your children. Preschoolers should not be allowed to handle the bird. They should be reminded not to stick their fingers in the cage. While it is important to set the limits of what they can't do, give your children opportunities to become acquainted with the cockatiel. Let them know that they will have an increasingly active role in the bird's care as they grow older and can handle the responsibility. Remember, cockatiels have a long life span and should be around for some time to come.

Problem Behaviors

Before you jump to the conclusion that your bird is misbehaving, check first to see if there could be a physical cause

for what is happening. Sometimes feather plucking, screaming, or biting is the result of a malady. Perhaps your bird's diet or environment is the cause of the problem.

After you've checked for any physical causes, you can then work on behavior modification techniques to correct these difficulties.

Biting—It's Not All Bad

When cockatiels are young, they go through a teething stage during which they will "beak" everything in sight. Just like a teething baby, everything goes into the mouth. As birds grow older, they may bite as a way of examining their environment. Often, before stepping on a new perch, a bird will test it out to see if it is strong enough for support by using his beak.

Examine your bird's body language to see if he is exhibiting any signs of aggression, such as flaring his wings or raising his crest. This signals that the bird is ready to bite. Try to redirect the

Many problem behaviors, like screaming, can be resolved by changing your cockatiel's environment or the physical condition that may be making him ill or uncomfortable.

Training Stubborn Birds

Positive reinforcement is the best method of getting your bird out of those entrenched behaviors that are either harmful to him or annoying to you. Birds are reward-motivated rather than punishment-driven. Avoid using punishment because it doesn't work with animals. To stop the undesirable behavior, you must take positive steps to redirect the behavior immediately or else the bird will not make the connection. Interest your bird in something else and then reward him for doing something positive. Always remember to be consistent as well as patient with your pet.

bird's behavior by offering him a toy to chew or directing him to a behavior that can be rewarded. Also examine your actions to see if you provoked the biting incident by moving too quickly and startling the bird.

Screaming

When your cockatiel starts to scream, your first reaction might be a negative one. You might be tempted to yell back. This, of course, is pointless. It will not change the behavior or make you feel better. Behavior modification is the key to stopping annoying actions. Try walking away for a few minutes to see if the screaming stops. Once it stops, give a reward for a different behavior. Since cockatiels are smart, it shouldn't be long before your pet realizes that a change in behavior will get your attention and a positive response.

Screeching will happen in the morning or in the evening. It can't be stopped altogether, but you should be able to break the habit during the day.

Chewing

A good rule of thumb is never assume. If you find that your bird is starting to chew on things in the house, examine this behavior to see if you can find a reason for the actions. Maybe your bird is trying to sharpen his beak. If that is the case, make sure you have mineral blocks or cuttlebones in the cage. If your cockatiel is chewing household things, and you find that there is no physiological reason for this behavior, try redirecting your bird to chew on appropriate items such as toys from the cage. It is important to watch that your pet is not chewing on anything that could be toxic or can lead to health problems.

Feather Plucking

An annoying behavior that can have serious consequences is self-mutilation or plucking. A bird might pluck a few feathers from himself, or he might pluck himself bare. While the cause of self-plucking is not clear, it is sometimes attributed to poor diet, skin diseases, parasites, poor environmental conditions, or emotional problems due to neglect. The emotional factor is often evidenced when cockatiels are confined to tiny cages with no human interaction. Fortunately, this condition is not common in cockatiels due to their placid, amiable natures.

Food Flinging

Cockatiels, like all hookbills, display one behavior that can be exasperating. They will often attack their food dishes looking for that "perfect tidbit," flinging seeds and pellets in all directions. Some birds are worse than others, but all birds will do it at times. Aside from the mess, a lot of food can be wasted.

There are several ways of combating this annoying habit to minimize the waste and the mess. One is to offer the various components of the diet in separate bowls — budgie mix in one, pellets in another, etc. Another method worth trying is only filling the food dish partially. This way the food will fling against the sides of the bowl rather than scatter all over the cage. Some pet stores now carry covered feed dishes with a hooded-top front opening.

Travel Carrier Training

At some point, you may decide to travel with your pet, or you may have to transport him for other reasons. Therefore, it's wise to acclimate your cockatiel to a travel carrier as soon as you are able. This should be done gradually. Since training should always be undertaken in small steps, begin by putting your cockatiel in the carrier for short periods of time. Reward him for going into the cage. Gradually build up to having the bird in it for longer periods of time. When he is used to the carrier, take it and put it in the car. Go for a short ride. Build up gradually to the next step when your bird seems ready. Then, when you have an emergency or your cockatiel has his yearly examination, being placed into the carrier won't stress or traumatize him.

Make training a part of your cockatiel's daily routine; not only will it reinforce what he learns, but it will provide exercise for both mind and body.

Resources

Clubs and Societies

American Federation of Aviculture
P.O. Box 7312
N. Kansas City, MO 64116
Phone: (816) 421-BIRD (2473)
Fax: (816) 421-3214
Website: www.AFAbirds.org

Association of Avian Veterinarians
P.O. Box 811720
Boca Raton, FL 33481
Phone: (561) 393-8901
Fax: (561) 393-8902
Website: www.aav.org

Avicultural Society of America
P.O. Box 5516
Riverside, CA 92517
Website: www.asabirds.org

National Cockatiel Society (NCS)
140 Almy Street
Warwick, RI 02886-3604
E-mail: membership@cockatiels.org or
nancyr@citilink.net
www.cockatiels.org

**North American Cockatiel Society
(NACS)**
P.O. Box 143
Bethel, CT 06801-0143
E-mail: membership@cockatiel.org or
walkkey@comcast.net
www.cockatiel.org

Veterinary Resources

**Academy of Veterinary
Homeopathy (AVH)**
P.O. Box 9280
Wilmington, DE 19809
http://www.theavh.org

**American Academy of Veterinary
Acupuncture (AAVA)**
66 Morris Avenue, Suite 2A
Springfield, NJ 07081
E-mail: office@aava.org
http://www.aava.org/

**American Animal Hospital
Association (AAHA)**
P.O. Box 150899
Denver, CO 80215-0899
E-mail: info@aahanet.org
http://www.aahanet.org/Index.cfm

**American College of Veterinary
Internal Medicine (ACVIM)**
1997 Wadsworth Blvd., Suite A
Lakewood, CO 80214-5293
Telephone: (800) 245-9081
Fax: (303) 231-0880
Email: ACVIM@ACVIM.org
www.acvim.org

American College of Veterinary Ophthalmologists (ACVO)
P.O. Box 1311
Meridian, Idaho 83860
Telephone: (208) 466-7624
Fax: (208) 466-7693
E-mail: office@acvo.com
www.acvo.com

American Holistic Veterinary Medical Association (AHVMA)
2218 Old Emmorton Road
Bel Air, MD 21015
E-mail: office@ahvma.org
http://www.ahvma.org/

American Veterinary Chiropractic Association (AVCA)
442154 E 140 Rd.
Bluejacket, OK 74333
Telephone: (918) 784-2231
E-mail: amvetchiro@aol.com
www.animalchiropractic.org

American Veterinary Medical Association (AVMA)
1931 North Meacham Road-Suite 100
Schaumburg, IL 60173
E-mail: avmainfo@avma.org
http://www.avma.org

**Animal Behavior Society
Indiana University
2611 East 10th Street #170
Bloomington IN 47408-2603**
Telephone: (812) 856-5541
E-mail: aboffice@indiana.edu
www.animalbehavior.org

Association of Avian Veterinarians (AAV)
P.O. Box 811720
Boca Raton, FL 33481-1720
Phone: (561) 393-8901
Fax: (561) 393-8902
AAVCTRLOFC@aol.com
www.aav.org

British Veterinary Association (BVA)
7 Mansfield Street
London
W1G 9NQ
Telephone: 020 7636 6541
Fax: 020 7436 2970
E-mail: bvahq@bva.co.uk
www.bva.co.uk

International Veterinary Acupuncture Society (IVAS)
P.O. Box 271395
Ft. Collins, CO 80527-1395
E-mail: office@ivas.org
http://www.ivas.org/main.cfm

Orthopedic Foundation for Animals (OFA)
2300 NE Nifong Blvd
Columbus, Missouri 65201-3856
Telephone: (573) 442-0418
Fax: (573) 875-5073
Email: ofa@offa.org
www.offa.org

Emergency Resources

ASPCA Animal Poison Control Center
Phone:(888) 426-4435
napcc@aspca.org (for general information only)
www.apcc.aspca.org

Bird Hotline
P.O. Box 1411
Sedona, AZ 86339-1411
birdhotline@birdhotline.com
www.birdhotline.com

Rescue and Adoption Agencies

American Humane Association (AHA)
63 Inverness Drive East
Englewood, CO 80112
Telephone: (303) 792-9900
Fax: 792-5333
www.americanhumane.org

American Society for the Prevention of Cruelty to Animals (ASPCA)
424 E. 92nd Street
New York, NY 10128-6804
Phone: (212) 876-7700
http://www.aspca.org

Bird Placement Program
P.O. Box 347392
Parma, OH, 44134-7392
Phone: (330) 772-1627
or (216) 749-3643
www.avi-sci.com/bpp/

Caged Bird Rescue
911 Thomson Road
Pegram, TN 37143
Phone: (615) 646-3949

Exotic Bird Rescue Ring
http://www.neebs.org/birdresc.htm

Feathered Friends Adoption and Rescue Program
East Coast Headquarters
4751 Ecstasy Circle
Cocoa, FL, 32926
Phone: (407) 633-4744
West Coast Branch
Phone: (941) 764-6048
http://members.aol.com/_ht_a/MAHort on/FFAP.html

Gabriel Foundation
P.O. Box 11477
Aspen, CO 81612
Phone: (877) 923-1009
www.thegabrielfoundation.org

The Humane Society of the United States (HSUS)
2100 L Street, NW
Washington DC 20037
Phone: (202) 452-1100
http://www.hsus.org

Index

Index

About the Author

Ellen Fusz, an avid animal lover, is a freelance writer and has published numerous articles and books, mostly for children. She also assisted in developing a pet-based website, PetFreedom.com. A veteran teacher of 31 years, Ellen has been honored for her work in education, including creating and writing educational materials and programs. She resides in St. Louis, Missouri, with her sister, Ann, and their three dogs.

Photo Credits